VARIETIES OF PARABLE

THE CLARK LECTURES

1963

VARIETIES OF PARABLE

BY

LOUIS MACNEICE

CAMBRIDGE

AT THE UNIVERSITY PRESS

1965

PUBLISHED BY

THE SYNDICS OF THE CAMBRIDGE UNIVERSITY PRESS

Bentley House, 200 Euston Road, London, N.W. 1
American Branch: 32 East 57th Street, New York, N.Y. 10022
West African Office: P.O. Box 33, Ibadan, Nigeria

©

CAMBRIDGE UNIVERSITY PRESS

1965

Printed in Great Britain at the University Printing House, Cambridge
(Brooke Crutchley, University Printer)

LIBRARY OF CONGRESS CATALOGUE
CARD NUMBER: 66-10036

PREFACE

LOUIS MACNEICE delivered these Clark Lectures in the spring of 1963, a few months before his death. Had he lived he would have polished and expanded them for publication. As it is, they are printed here with no more than the necessary minimum of editorial revision. A short bibliography has been added.

The publishers would like to take the opportunity to acknowledge the help of Professor E. R. Dodds in seeing the proofs through the press.

CONTENTS

INTRODUCTION

W HAT is to be the subject of these lectures? I have called them *Varieties of Parable* but with some misgiving; I don't like the word 'parable' and it suggests something much too narrow for my purpose, namely the parables of the New Testament. On the other hand the other possible words seemed even less satisfactory. 'Symbolism' for instance has been vastly over-used and to some critics a symbol means something very plastic while to others it means something quite rigid. As for the adjective 'symbolical', it is a notorious get-out or let-out word, used by authors when they want to get away with a murder they're not quite sure they have committed. At the same time the word is too wide in its reference: in language at least it is not possible not to use symbols, since all language, on ultimate analysis, is by its nature symbolical. But in these lectures I hope, wherever possible, to avoid ultimate analysis.

Then there is 'allegory' but this is a word to which many people today are allergic and if one uses it too widely one has no word left for the category of allegory proper. 'Fable', to me at least, suggests a miniature, such as the fables of Aesop, with a painfully obvious moral and usually written in a shown-to-the-children manner. I did think of using 'fantasy', which should be wide enough—almost too wide, though it would exclude the New Testament parables—but which suffers from the pejorative associations of Coleridge's 'Fancy'; I notice that Mr Kingsley Amis in a book about science fiction, which he approves of, is at pains to distinguish it from fantasy, which he dislikes. Lastly there is 'myth', which because of its pedigree and its religious implications is far and away the noblest of these words. One often hears people nowadays—and I agree with them—regretting the deficiency of myth in modern poetry. On the other hand, if the word is used strictly, myth is something that the will cannot supply, for it has to be given or rather inherited (though Jungians would no doubt maintain that the myths are always there waiting in the Collective Unconscious; unfortunately this, like any other unconscious, is not a reservoir anyone can tap at will). Anyhow, 'myth' does not seem to me the right word to cover some of the works I want to cover, such as *Alice in Wonderland*, the novels of William Golding and the plays of Harold Pinter. But all these, I think, can be squeezed under the umbrella of 'parable'.

According to the *Oxford Dictionary*, 'parable' means 'any saying or narration in which something is expressed in terms of something else'. 'Also,' it adds, 'any kind of enigmatical or dark saying.' This should certainly cover the whole range of my specimens from the *Faerie Queene*, which Spenser himself described as a 'dark conceit', to *The Ancient Mariner*, *Waiting for Godot*, *Pincher Martin* or the poems of Edwin Muir. Within this range there will naturally fall some works that can be labelled with my discarded words and can be correctly described, in whole or in part, as allegories, fantasies and so on. But, to counter the 'dark saying' of the dictionary, I should like to anticipate some of my later remarks and state baldly here that one very valuable kind of parable, and particularly so today, is the kind which on the surface may not look like a parable at all. This is a kind of double-level writing, or, if you prefer it, sleight-of-hand. It has been much used by poets and one could make out a case that all worthwhile poetry involves something of the sort. However, I shall not attempt to make any such case here as I want to keep the subject within limits, even though those limits must be arbitrary. Thus I am prepared to squeeze in Wordsworth's leech-gatherer but not, say, Browning's bishop who orders his tomb. Similarly, in the novel, while I should admit Melville's white whale, I should exclude the bulls and big game of Hemingway, even though a case could quite well be made for their inclusion. I am also excluding works which may contain one large and recurrent symbol but which are otherwise written in a naturalistic mode. Examples of such works are Chekhov's *The Seagull* and Miss Iris Murdoch's novel *The Bell*, in both of which title and symbol coincide. I am not so sure, however, about another work where the title gives the symbol, Ibsen's *The Wild Duck*. This, like several of Ibsen's so-called 'naturalistic' plays, does seem to function on two levels continuously and consistently.

This question of double-level writing brings me to a distinction which, thanks to Freud in particular, was very fashionable when I left school in the 1920's, the distinction between 'manifest' and 'latent' content. We also kept harping on the distinctions between 'statement' and 'suggestion' and between 'denotation' and 'connotation', but the manifest–latent one went deeper than these. In all three distinctions one is of course concerned not only with content but with form. In *The Allegory of Love* Professor C. S. Lewis, echoing while inverting the Elizabethan

3

rhetoric books which defined allegory as 'a continued Metaphore' or 'a long and perpetuall Metaphore', writes: 'We cannot speak, perhaps we can hardly think, of an "inner conflict" without a metaphor; and every metaphor is an allegory in little.' Now within any work the relative importance of a metaphor or image to the thing imaged is very difficult to assess. (It has been pointed out—correctly, I think—that even a negative simile or comparison can add something to a poem: where Milton writes, '*Not* that fair field of Enna' could compete with the Garden of Eden, he is, to some extent, Sicilianizing Eden.) But the relative weight of a single image will depend upon the size of the work which contains it: in a short lyric such an image can be the focal point of the whole. In long works, such as plays, to make a comparable impact the image or, more probably, a number of images of the same type must keep recurring. George Wilson Knight made a study of this process in the case of *Othello*. Imagery, then, can modify the manifest content and reinforce the latent content. However, not only imagery can do this but all other formal elements of a literary work—for instance, tone of voice or syntax or rhythm—three things which will be found, in Samuel Beckett for one, to be not only formal but constituent of meaning.

For this reason, though I regard Professor Lewis as our greatest connoisseur of allegory, I would disagree with him when he says: 'Symbolism is a mode of thought, but allegory is a mode of expression.' Allegory, except at its most naïve or banal, is such a strong mode of expression that I would expect any thought expressed by it to be modified by it. I prefer here Dr Janet Spens's remark, when discussing

Spenser's symbolism, that for the Elizabethans 'Abstractions were warm with Personality'. And Professor Lewis himself seems to undermine his own contention when he writes: 'Allegory, in some senses, belongs not to medieval man, but to man, or even to mind, in general.' He also writes that allegory came 'to supply the *subjective* element in literature', and how the subjective element can be divorced from thought I find it hard to conceive. But this whole awkward and confusing opposition of allegory and symbolism has been helpfully discussed by Mr Graham Hough in a recently published book, *A Preface to the Faerie Queene*, so I shall leave it over till I come to Mr Hough's 'graduated scale' of all kinds of creative writing from allegory to near-documentary.

I doubt whether one can draw a clear distinction, as Professor Lewis did, between a mode of expression and a mode of thought. As every poet knows, one cannot draw any clear line between form and content. Yet, as every critic knows, without drawing such a line criticism is impossible. So, just as with any other kind of writing, in order to discuss parable writing at all one has to use what Aristotle would call a 'bastard reasoning' and pretend that form and content can be separated. Let us take then six writers of parable— Spenser, Bunyan, Kafka, Beckett, Harold Pinter and William Golding—and ask what they have in common as regards content. The obvious answer is that they all create special worlds. This is most obvious in *The Faerie Queene*; but then that is written in verse and in all such works, whatever Wordsworth may say, the very fact that they are in verse removes them from the everyday world. The other five have a deceptive matter-of-factness, but each of them creates a special world, and what is interesting in each case is to look for the relationship between that and the ordinary world, or in other words to examine the amount—or the kind—of realism they exhibit.

In Bunyan, for instance, the allegory is most consistent and manifest. In spite of that the characters keep assuming the features and voices of the solid townsfolk of seventeenth-century Bedford. Kafka, on the other hand, is quite obviously caricaturing *his* contemporary world but in the process he lifts it—or rather lowers it—to the plane of an admittedly very sinister fairy story. Pinter in his plays does something similar: his highly naturalistic dialogue contrives at the same time both to belie and to underpin his perhaps hardly conscious symbolism. Golding in his first three novels, *The Lord of the Flies*, *The Inheritors* and *Pincher Martin*, each of which is a *tour de force*, produces three different special worlds each of which would serve, though in quite different ways, as a parable of the human situation today. *The Lord of the Flies* approaches Kafka, in that its island run by little boys is a frightening parody of modern society. *Pincher Martin* approaches Beckett in that the whole drama here is that of a solitary individual facing his doom and coming to grips with life at the moment of death. Both of these are set in the contemporary world. *The Inheritors*, on the other hand, is set in the Stone Age, which is at least as far away from us as Spenser's Faerie Land. With Golding, as with Spenser, this fact of sheer distance makes the moral stand out more clearly. Once we have watched his apish Neanderthalers fascinated and frightened by the people who are superseding them, our own transitional period, stripped of its topical bric-a-brac, looms up through the primeval forest with stronger outlines and increased significance. All six of these writers have something paradoxical about them, which I shall try to pin down later, merely suggesting here that our own times seem to predispose writers to paradox. For the time being I will rest on the generalization that the writer of parable literature, whether it is novel, short story, poem or play, is, by contrast with other types of writer, engaged in projecting a special world.

To leave these generalizations for the moment, I will commit myself personally. This dubious ground which I am exploring attracted me in three of my capacities, as a person, as a poet and as a practitioner in sound radio. As a person I have from childhood been a steady dreamer (I mean in the literal sense) and I have never been tempted to dismiss dreams as 'insubstantial' or 'unreal'; long before I read the psychologists, I took it for granted that my dreams had a lot to do with me myself and with my world. Also, unless I deceived myself and groomed my dreams on waking, I remember in all periods of my life having dreams which had a fair degree of shape. These dreams were often akin to fairy stories, and real fairy stories have always meant much to me as a person, even when I was at a public school where to admit this meant losing face. Contrary to what many people say even now, a fairy story, at least of the classical folk variety, is a much more solid affair than the average naturalistic novel, whose roots go little deeper than a gossip column. From folk tales and sophisticated fairy tales such as Hans Andersen's and various legends from Greek or Norse mythology and freak works like the Alice books and *Water Babies* I graduated, at about the age of twelve, to *The Faerie Queene*. And this brings me to the second of the three capacities in which I am drawn to what I call parable writing.

In poetry as a reader I have fairly catholic tastes but I would rather read Spenser than most: this is because of his exceptional depth and variety and because his work has the richness and complexity of the best dreams and the truth to life of the best fairy stories. In poetry as a writer I have more often than not worked at the opposite pole to Spenser, confining myself largely (no poet can confine himself completely) to the external world and therefore at times becoming a journalist rather than a creative writer. In the 1930's we used to say that the poet should contain the journalist; now I would tend more often to use 'contain' in the sense of control or limit. I still hold that a poet should look at, feel about and think about the world around him, but he should not suppose his job consists merely in reporting on it. What the poet is far more concerned with is that 'inner conflict' mentioned by Professor Lewis which he said requires metaphorical writing. So in English poetry I was sorry to see a few years ago that movement which was called The Movement deliberately lowering its sights and concentrating on neat observations within a very limited sphere. Oddly enough, at about the same time various playwrights were taking up what the poets were letting go. I shall come back to this. What I myself would now like to write, if I could, would be double-level poetry, of the type of Wordsworth's 'Resolution and Independence', and, secondly, more overt parable poems in a line of descent both from folk ballads such as 'True Thomas' and some of George Herbert's allegories in miniature such as 'Redemption'.

8

Thirdly, I said that I was attracted to parable forms as a practitioner in sound radio. Here it was the medium itself propelling me. For, where television is more likely to propel one in the opposite direction, to an extreme, if limited, form of naturalism, sound radio, thanks to the lack of any visual element, is very well able, when attempting fantasy, to achieve the necessary suspension of disbelief. Many traditional fairy stories, for example, have been successfully dramatized and produced in this medium, as has *Everyman*. Apart from such adaptations of existing material, it tempts one, more than the stage does and far more than television, to experiment in modern morality plays or parable plays. I myself have had several shots at this but only once, I think, to my own satisfaction. The 'morality' type of play is particularly difficult because, when writing for a mass audience, it is unlikely that a writer today will share the necessary moral framework with them. And most kinds of fantasy, particularly satirical fantasy, are today, it is said, caviare to the general. Thus in the cinema, which unlike television can support fantasy, we are told that the films made by Cocteau and Ingmar Bergman could never conceivably be 'box office'. But that Bergman 'film festivals' can be organized in England does seem to prove that there are a fair number of people for whom this kind of work fills an emotional need. I would qualify this by pointing out that Bergman, in *Through a Glass Darkly*, dropped the overt fantasy or supernatural elements; there was nothing here like the shot in *Wild Strawberries* where the wheel of the hearse passes the wrong side of the lamp-post without coming off, and yet Bergman contrives to be as sombre and haunting as ever. There is a parallel in the

9

plays of Harold Pinter whose *Birthday Party* and *The Caretaker*, without losing any of the menace, dispense with the obvious melodrama of his first play *The Room* and with the supernatural mechanics of his second play *The Dumb Waiter*. In sleight-of-hand writing an *apparent* straight-forwardness is often a great asset; Beckett uses it too. On the other hand, as I shall maintain when I come to Bunyan, in what would otherwise be naïve allegory it is a plain athletic style and especially naturalistic dialogue that give it a third dimension.

As a child I took among other things to Greek and Norse mythology. Curiously, since I lived in Ireland, I was not offered the early Irish legends but I doubt if I would have taken to them with equal enthusiasm. Traditional legends of this kind will not come into this survey—I am only dealing with conscious or deliberate works of literature—but this distinction may be significant. There is plenty of pretty crude fantasy in Greek and even more in Norse mythology but most of it is acceptable, at least to a child, because one can see the point of it. Saturn has a good reason for eating his children and anyhow is behaving like any familiar ogre in the folk tales, and the role of ogre can easily be imposed on any father. The Valkyries and the Twilight of the Gods are both intelligible and exciting to a normal child, and many of the legends in both cultures are moving—the Rape of Persephone and the Death of Balder. But it is different when one turns to Celtic legend. The pre-eminent ancient Irish hero is Cuchulain; Yeats tried throughout his life to make something of him. But Cuchulain was unpromising material except—to the modern mind—for grotesque farce, an opportunity which was seized by Flann O'Brien in his extraordinary book *At-Swim-Two-Birds*. What happens to Cuchulain when he gets into his battle frenzy? He twists himself inside his skin so that his heels and buttocks appear in front. One eye goes back into his head and the other protrudes enormous and red. His hair bristles and on each single hair is a drop of blood. And a column of dark blood rises from the top of his head like the mast of a great ship. And so on: they called him 'The Contorted One'. What happens again when he is showing off to women? He suddenly sports four spots—yellow, green, blue and purple —on each cheek, seven fingers on each hand, seven toes on each foot and seven pupils in each eye. All this interests analysts of racial mythologies; an analysis of such material has recently been made by Alwyn and Brinley Rees in their book *Celtic Heritage*. But it is not the best material for a modern poet or playwright, and I bring it in here as an example of the sort of fantasy I am not concerned with. Of course some poet or playwright might use the Rees brothers' interpretations of it in the way Mr Eliot used Jessie Weston's *From Ritual to Romance*, but so far no one has done this.

To be fair, I must now add that there *are* Celtic legends which in their own right, without gloss or analysis, can excite our sense of mystery or sympathy. Such are the old Irish Voyages. We can't 'identify', as they say, with Cuchulain but it is easy to identify with St Brandon and the others in their adventures on the western sea. The longest of these stories, The Voyage of Maeldúin, was used by Tennyson as the basis for a poem. In the original the hero, who is intelligibly engaged in a vendetta, is blown out to sea and comes to thirty-one islands, one after the other. These, or some of them, as can be seen from Tennyson's poem, are what could be called parable islands: thus there is an island corresponding to Homer's island of Lotos-eaters and another, the 'Isle of Witches', corresponding to those of Circe and Calypso. There is also, more original and more seemingly modern in its menace, an island, in the words of the Rees brothers, 'whose people shout "It is they!" at the voyagers, as though they knew of their coming and feared them'. Such a voyage, like any form of quest, has an immemorial place in legend. And the theme crops up again and again in sophisticated literature: look at *The Ancient Mariner*. The great majority of folk tales include journeys, sometimes on sea, more often on land, and the quest which in such stories is usually aimed at finding a fortune or a bride can become in other hands the Quest of the Grail or of the City of Zion.

I have mentioned folk tales and traditional myths because my early pleasure in them predisposed me in favour of the various kinds of writing which I mean to discuss and because these kinds of writing, much though they may differ from each other, seem often to display the virtues which are found in the folk tales and the myths. A play with so little action as *Waiting for Godot* may not, on the surface, appear very like a folk tale, but in the qualities of suspense, mystery and inevitability, as also in the tit-for-tat nature of its dialogue, it is much more like one than it is like, say, a novel by Fielding or Jane Austen or John Wain, or a play by Wilde or Shaw or John Osborne, or indeed the bulk of our literature.

In the following chapters I shall discuss five groups of works, roughly determined by period. The first will include Spenser and Bunyan: they are enormously different from each other but they do have some things in common and I find both their differences and their similarities illuminating. At the same time I shall glance at George Herbert. The second group I call, loosely, the Romantics. Coleridge and Shelley will of course come in here, and also Blake, but I shall also look back to some of the traditional ballads and forward to Christina Georgina Rossetti who, though she wrote some very moving lyrics, also wrote one very bad allegorical poem, 'The Prince's Progress'. A bad poem like this may throw light on the nature of parable. In the third group my major exhibits will be nineteenth-century books for children by authors like Lewis Carroll, Charles Kingsley and George MacDonald, but I shall look forward as far as or beyond the turn of the century to people who might be considered forerunners of those modern poets, playwrights and novelists who are the subject of my two last groups.

Two books have recently appeared which I have found very relevant and helpful: *The Theatre of the Absurd* by Martin Esslin and *A Preface to the Faerie Queene* by Graham Hough. Both these authors are enthusiasts; and as I largely share their two very different enthusiasms, and as between them they cover a good deal of my ground, I shall at this point give a brief summary of their main theses.

While I share Esslin's admiration for playwrights like Beckett and Pinter, I do not go the whole way with his generalizations. He seems to assume that when people lose belief in God they also have to give up discursive thought and logic. He too often boosts his 'Theatre of the Absurd' by sneering at 'drawing-room comedy'—as if there were nothing in between. He perceives and appears to approve of a 'devaluation of language': 'Language appears more and more as being in contradiction to reality.' At the same time he is somewhat subservient to the psychologists: 'the sub-conscious has a higher content of reality than the conscious utterance'. He sometimes uses the word 'reality' rather too easily. And he seems to endorse what he calls 'Beckett's intuition that *nothing really ever happens* in man's existence'. 'In this', he goes on, 'the Theatre of the Absurd is analo-gous to a Symbolist or Imagist poem.' Mr Hough could have pointed out to him the limitations of Imagism (it is not at all surprising that it has joined the dead movements) and Esslin has done his favourites no service by dragging in this analogy. On the other hand I do agree with him that the Theatre of the Absurd is 'essentially lyrical'. Where most playwrights throughout history have been concerned with problems in the external world which admit of an answer, these playwrights are now doing what poets have done so often, putting the age-old unanswerable questions: Why am I here? Who am I? What is the purpose of it all? As Esslin sees, merely to put such a question can bring about something very like catharsis. But only if you put it effectively, as in a successful lyric.

Esslin, I think, goes too far in postulating the peculiarity of the modern world. Thus he seems to regard 'the madness of the times' as unprecedented and comments: 'No wonder that the art of such an era shows a marked resemblance to the symptoms of schizophrenia.' But in fact the one really peculiar thing in our world is the Bomb; and as Arthur Koestler has pointed out, however much we have realized the implications of that with our heads, we have not yet *grown into* that realization: the possibility of death for the whole human race is not something we live with as we live with the certainty of our own individual deaths. Anyhow Esslin does not seem to be concerned with the Bomb. He starts from the Existentialist starting-point but feels that the Existentialists themselves did not live up to their own preaching: Sartre and Camus in their plays 'express the new content in the old convention'; whereas 'the Theatre of the Absurd strives to express its sense of the senselessness of the human condition and the inadequacy of the rational approach by the open abandonment of rational devices and discursive thought'. So *Huis Clos*, because its form is not matched to its content, is inferior to *Endgame*. But Esslin's contention here can at least be disputed: Mr Eliot's theory, put forward in 1921, that in a dislocated world poetry must be dislocated too, has been disputed now for several decades.

Most of Mr Esslin's playwrights are atheists but I feel he is right in finding in their work 'a return to the original, religious function of the theatre'. When Esslin talks about the 'religious element' in these plays he does not mean anything to do with dogma, which he thinks today belongs to the domain of science. He means two things: first, and far the more important, a mystical sense of man's position in the universe (even if it is an unbearable position, to grasp this is somehow to transcend it) and, second, that these playwrights use the theatre in the way the Church used ritual. In all countries and in all ages mystics have tended to express themselves in terms of the Ineffable and as creators and communicators they may be allowed to get away with this contradiction in terms. But critics should be wary of the word. I suspect that it is his obsession with the Ineffable that makes Mr Esslin keep harping on the 'devaluation of language' which he finds in such an author as Beckett. He seems to think that the mime and the silences in Beckett's plays are just as important as the words. I beg to differ: the silences, at least in my opinion, are there to throw the words into relief. And, in advancing this thesis, he seems to forget that Beckett has not only written plays. He has written a number of prose narratives—though narrative is perhaps not quite the right word for them—which stand or fall by the words alone: in my opinion they stand—and for the simple reason that Beckett is a master of words. A long monologue like *Malone Dies* has been properly described as a prose poem. Esslin was on surer ground when he wrote that the Theatre of the Absurd is essentially lyrical.

The extraordinary paradoxes permeating, not to say constituting, the work of such a writer as Beckett are to be discussed later. But having now flourished a few samples of such paradoxes I think it is time, for the sake of clarity, to call in Mr Hough. In *A Preface to the Faerie Queene* his main subject is of course Spenser, about whom he is highly perceptive. In one chapter of this book, however, entitled 'Allegory in *The Faerie Queene*', he branches out into a very much wider field. Here, inspired by the example of Northrop Frye's 'Theory of Symbols' in *The Anatomy of Criticism*, he works out a graduated scale for all creative writing. To represent this by a diagram he puts forward a circular instead of a linear arrangement. He has been driven to formulate this very ingenious scheme by discontent with the traditional antithesis of 'symbolism' and 'allegory' as formulated by such despisers of the latter as Blake, Coleridge, and Yeats. Hough finds that 'a metaphysical spectre' has been lurking behind this distinction. It is odd, as he remarks, that Blake, who instead of saying 'symbolism' says 'Vision', should admit that allegory, which he much despises, is 'seldom without some Vision' and that '*Pilgrim's Progress* is full of it'. If the two are so intertwined, 'surely', as Hough says, 'the opposition between the two has been made too absolute'. Hough then postulates a third kind of writing, based on the simple perception of a pattern in events, such as that shown in any Rake's Progress. But, if there are more than two kinds, there are also more than three. And so he moves on to his circular scheme.

Mr Hough's scheme is based upon the varying ratio between two elements, which he calls 'theme' and 'image': he uses '"theme" for the moral or metaphysical "abstract" element . . . and "image" for the "concrete" characters, actions or objects in which it is embodied'. So he starts from the fact that there are two 'extremes, literature in which theme is dominant, and literature in which image is dominant'. The first of these extremes is represented by 'naïve allegory' (he has borrowed this phrase from Northrop Frye), which on the clockface of his circle he places at twelve o'clock. In this kind of writing what Hough calls 'image' is completely subservient and 'we are on the verge of passing out of literature altogether', e.g. into political propaganda. (I shall discuss later why *Pilgrim's Progress* cannot be classified as 'naïve allegory'.) The other extreme, where 'image' is dominant, stands at six o'clock and here we are 'on the edge of passing out of literature into reporting': Hough gives this kind of writing the name of 'realism'. Halfway between these two, at three o'clock, stands Shakespeare in whom 'theme and image seem equally balanced': Hough calls this sort of writing 'incarnational' on the grounds that here 'any "abstract" content is completely absorbed in character and action and completely expressed by them'. Between Shakespeare at three o'clock and the near-rapportage of six o'clock fall the majority of novels. There are some freak novels which fall in the first quarter while there are some second-quarter novels, such as those of Dickens, which include marked first-quarter elements. But going backwards, between Shakespeare at three o'clock and the discursive writing of twelve o'clock fall most of the works I shall be discussing in these lectures. Hough places about one o'clock 'allegory proper' such as *The Faerie Queene* and about two o'clock what Northrop Frye calls 'free-style allegory'—such works as Goethe's *Faust* and *Peer Gynt*. He also would place in this quarter such things as the Comedy of Humours where events or characters evince a recognizable pattern.

As for the second half of Hough's circle, the hours between six and twelve, they are not so relevant to my purpose. At half-past seven Hough places Imagism, where the images 'engage in mysterious correspondences and enter into occult relations with vision'. At nine o'clock he places 'symbolism' which, like the plays of Shakespeare on the opposite side of the clockface, 'seeks for the union of theme and image' but, in Hough's view, not so successfully. The attempt seems to be made in two ways, either by using words as talismans, or, like Blake, in setting out 'to *see* the invisible with all the concreteness of sense-experience'. And at half-past ten he places what he calls Emblem or Hieratic Symbolism: here the symbolism tends to become fixed—'the image shrinks and becomes stereotyped, and theme expands'. Hieratic symbolism, Hough says, 'exists largely outside literature,' but he instances Yeats as a poet who often used imagery in this way. I am not so happy about Hough's second half of the circle but then nor is Hough himself. However, accepting this formulation as at least serviceable, I would point out that, while most of my chosen works of parable fall in the first quarter of the clockface, in fact between 12.0 and 2.0 or 2.30 rather than 3.0, since none of them achieves Shakespeare's balance of theme and image, there are places in most of these works where almost any hour can strike—or at least appear to strike. As I said before, I shall try to investigate the element of 'realism' in parable (in Pinter for example). This is just one of several questions which will crop up recurrently. Among others are the following.

First, the question of Belief. This, as always, is a puzzler. We have all met people who maintain very blithely that it makes no difference to the appreciation of Dante whether one is a Christian—let alone a Catholic—or a non-Christian. I have never felt at all sure about this and I certainly do not think one can appreciate the 'poetry' of Dante unless one is at least interested in the beliefs expressed in that poetry. Purely aesthetic evaluations may be possible with music or the visual arts but I doubt if that can ever be true of literary works. Anyhow, whereas I was implying before that in poetry the formal elements are part of the meaning or the content, I would add at this point that the content, which includes of course any beliefs expressed in a poem, must *ipso facto*—at least if that poem is to be valid—have a part in the shaping of that poem. Which means that in this respect the beliefs are formalizing elements.

I shall not discuss Dante, but in the next chapter I shall be discussing two great writers, the first of whom, Spenser, though not particularly either mystical or propagandist, remained essentially Christian both in his ethics and in his cosmology, and the second of whom, Bunyan, was essentially an evangelical writer, whose interests, unlike Spenser's, were entirely bound up with his creed. Now with English readers, I have noticed, their reactions to Bunyan are often quite different from their professed reactions to Dante. Faced with the spokesman of Thomist Catholicism they are very ready to say that his beliefs are irrelevant and that they can enjoy his poetry with the next man. But faced with the spokesman of the English Puritan Revolution they shy away in horror and say they just cannot stomach a writer who held such beliefs: this time it is not the beliefs but the beauty of the writing that is irrelevant. I suggest that the reason for this is that Bunyan is too near to us. Whatever his religion or lack of religion, every Englishman has to some degree inherited the Puritan Revolution just as he has inherited the Industrial Revolution. Therefore he can understand Bunyan much more easily than he can Dante and that is just what frightens him. For, if Bunyan's beliefs are not his, Bunyan's *experience* to some degree must be.

Perhaps indeed in creative works of literature the question of belief merges into the question of experience. And somewhere in between these two, or compounded of both, comes attitude. If we turn to a work both aesthetically and morally far inferior to *The Divine Comedy* and *Pilgrim's Progress*, namely to Charles Kingsley's *Water Babies*, we find that the beliefs and/or the attitude of the writer have to be considered not only under the heading of content but also under the heading of form. *Water Babies* is a grotesquely uneven book but its unevenness is an essential part of it. Kingsley had a marvellous central idea—Jungians could well call it archetypal—but I doubt if he would have got it launched if it had not been for his peculiar blend of muscular Christianity, jingoism, a passion for natural history and a kind of half-mystical, half-sentimental pantheism. For the last-named quality, it would illustrate the recurrence of ideas in very different kinds of parable writing to compare—and contrast—Kingsley's Mother Carey 'making things make themselves' with Spenser's 'Old Genius' in the Garden of Adonis:

> A thousand thousand naked babes attend
> About him day and night, which doe require
> That he with fleshly weedes would them attire . . .

My point here, however, is to stress that you should not approach a work like *Water Babies* as if it had come into being in a vacuum: like most of the more interesting so-called 'children's books' it is essentially adult, and an awareness of Victorian conflicts and, at the least, a suspension of antipathy towards its author's attitude will give weight to what otherwise might be written off as whimsical.

Before leaving this triple question of belief, experience and attitude, I would ask as a coda: What about unbelief? The playwrights discussed by Martin Esslin are for the most part diehard unbelievers and, if they have any positive philosophy, it is the anti-philosophy of existentialism. Here again, I think, the reader need not agree with them but he must share enough of their experience to be able to get on their wavelength. When *The Waste Land* was published, most of Mr Eliot's seniors just could not see the point of it.

People who have grown up since the war just cannot see the point of much of the poetry of the 1930's. In the same way I suspect that unless one had lived in France during the German occupation, it would be difficult to get the full value out of the writings of Sartre.

The question of belief–experience–attitude leads on to the question of enduring validity. Surface writings—cinematic reporting, naturalistic novels, comedies of manners—can be read long afterwards for their so-called 'period interest'. Parable writing, on the other hand, being imbued with the true inner feel of its period, may not be properly comprehensible or likeable to a reader who lacks knowledge of its historical background. This is why would-be readers of *The Romance of the Rose* or the poems of George Herbert should be so grateful, respectively, to C. S. Lewis and Rosamond Tuve. Much of Herbert indeed is straightforward enough to make some impact on anyone, regardless of his knowledge of Herbert's background. The reader's experience, however, will be greatly enriched if he knows something of what Miss Tuve calls the 'whole system of traditional and publicly known correspondences' implicit in much of Herbert's imagery. It is the same with Spenser: The Cave of Despair is universal and so are the lovely ladies like Amoret and Florimell (whose sheer sex appeal proves that they are not purely allegorical) but there is much in *The Faerie Queene* which may fall flat or even repel unless one is acquainted with the Elizabethan world-picture.

Here I might mention 'identification' and 'alienation'. Esslin finds a truer kind of 'alienation' in the Theatre of the Absurd than he does in the plays of Brecht who made 'alienation' a principle. For Esslin it is impossible to identify oneself with, say, the characters of Beckett. I disagree since I find this only too easy. I could certainly 'identify', as they say, with either of the tramps in *Waiting for Godot* or, disgusting though he is, with Krapp in *Krapp's Last Tape*. And in Pinter I could identify with any one of the three characters in *The Caretaker*. In the same way, in the world today, it is easy to identify with K. and Joseph K. in Kafka's *The Castle* and *The Trial*, or with the central characters in Golding's novels, including the Neanderthal man, Lok, who seems perfectly relevant to our modern situation.

Other questions will be concerned with the relation of form to content. It is noticeable, for instance, that most of my playwrights and novelists and also, among my poets, George Herbert, go in for a plain style. 'So he took him by the hand again, and led him into a very dark room, where there sat a man in an iron cage.' The plainness is like a truth drug or, putting it differently, the knife that almost killed the writer will cut the reader to the bone. Another example from Bunyan shows how the very naturalistic dialogue often found in parable writing serves to keep the balance between what Hough calls 'image' and 'theme'. *Pilgrim's Progress* ran the risk of being a dull dressed-up sermon but it cannot possibly be that while the people in it talk like Mrs Timorous, 'Well, I see you have a mind to go a-fooling too, but take heed in time, and be wise. While we are out of danger we are out; but when we are in, we are in.' A third example from Bunyan, this time from *The Holy War*, will illustrate how quite broad satire can often be integrated into a deeply felt piece of parable. It may also remind us that the devout and uneducated Bunyan was in some sense a successor to the erudite and worldly creator of Sir Politick Would-be and Sir Epicure Mammon. Here is Bunyan—a thumbnail note but a damning one. He has just introduced a Mr Wet-Eyes: 'Now this Wet-Eyes was a near neighbour of Mr Desires, a poor man, a man of a broken spirit, yet one that could speak well to a petition.' In some modern writers, such as Beckett, this satirical element, or on occasions an odd kind of slapstick humour, can get inextricably intertwined with the lyrical element remarked upon by Esslin.

A simpler question is the assessment of the story element —or the lack of it. In all traditional legends and folk tales and in *Pilgrim's Progress* and *Faust* and *Peer Gynt* and *The Lord of the Flies* a great deal happens in the course of the story, which makes it, in the popular sense, a good story. In Kafka, on the other hand, comparatively little happens and the hero is a sufferer rather than an agent. In Beckett— both the narrative works and the plays—action has almost disappeared. So what has Beckett in common with Bunyan or Ibsen? Quite a lot, I think, as I hope to show later. But there are also mixed types of parable such as *The Faerie Queene*. At a casual glance this seems to be full of story— or stories—but as various scholars, including Lewis and Hough, have pointed out, you have only to compare Spenser with Ariosto to see that in *The Faerie Queene* the story is not the point. It is situation—meaning inner situation—that counts, rather than the sequence of events. This is also the case with Beckett.

Here we come to 'character'. For the last two centuries the portrayal of character has dominated the novel and the theatre and it is only in the last few generations that a considerable reaction set in against it. This reaction was found in a number of quite different quarters, had a variety of motivations and was expressed from a variety of angles. Yeats, for example, wanted character kicked out of the drama but this was for the sake of a 'poetic' theatre very different from that of Mr Esslin's heroes. Then there were people—and are people—who play down character in order to play up story. But to the admirers of Beckett 'story', at any rate in the sense of plot, is almost a dirty word. Beckett, says Esslin, is working 'at a level where neither characters nor plot exist'. For myself this level is the *ne plus ultra*; I cannot see how anyone can out-Beckett Beckett. He stands at one extreme of parable writing. Between him and the writers of allegories of action there is a very wide range of literature. But, wide though its range is, parable writing is today the concern of only a minority. It is a growing minority and, I think, a very important one. This is why I am attempting to bring so many different strands together. There is something in the world today that makes me turn back to Spenser. And Spenser for me can throw light on Beckett or Golding. Perhaps the converse is also true.

II

SPENSER AND BUNYAN

IN talking about Spenser and Bunyan, I have to confess that I go back to these writers with ulterior motives. In the twentieth century, it seems to me, realism in the photographic sense is almost played out and no longer satisfies our needs. The writers who do seem pertinent are those like Kafka, Samuel Beckett and William Golding who, in their very different ways, practise some kind of what I have called parable writing. There is not, in the sense of literary influences, a direct line of descent to such writers from Spenser and Bunyan: my point is that they are doing the same kind of thing. For at least two centuries the realists were dominant. Today they are still the favourite reading of the majority, though even the majority gladly accept certain kinds of parable, in the field of science fiction, for instance: a book like *The Day of the Triffids* seems to me closer to Spenser than to the main tradition of the English novel.

What is very noticeable is that the parabolists, though still a minority and only accepted by a minority, have been steadily gaining ground. A few years ago it would have been inconceivable that plays like *Waiting for Godot* or *The Caretaker* should have been staged in the West End of London. With this one can correlate the renewed interest in such forms as allegory shown by critics on both sides of the Atlantic. Hough begins his *A Preface to the Faerie Queene* with the complaint that 'Spenser has been the most neglected of all our great poets in this century' but I feel myself that this neglect has for some time been on the wane. As long ago as 1936 C. S. Lewis in *The Allegory of Love* did a great deal to demonstrate that Spenser, far from being a mere decorator or escapist or fantasist in the narrow sense, was a very serious writer, essentially concerned with the realities of human life. Today across the Atlantic we find scholars like Northrop Frye and Rosamond Tuve and Edwin Honig taking it as axiomatic that reality at its deeper levels can be probed in literature only by something in the nature of what I am calling 'parable'.

I have suggested that any parable writer, in whatever form, is concerned with the projecting of a special world. How far such a special world must be also a private world is open to argument. In many modern novels and plays there is an obvious relation between the special world and the ordinary or everyday world in which history forces us to live. Sometimes, as in Kafka, Ionesco and Pinter, the relationship becomes one of parody, as it was in *Gulliver's Travels*. But often, both in novels and in plays, and most frequently in poetry, the author is dealing not with man the political or social animal, who is the one we can parody, but with man the solitary animal. In these latter cases the special world tends to become a private world. But even if this is so, it need not mean we cannot share it with its creator. Given the same historical and geographical background, many people's privacies tend to overlap. This has not only been proved by the psychologists, whether Freudian or Jungian, but was maintained even by a Marxist critic, Christopher Caudwell, in the objectivist, over-topical 1930's. Caudwell, who quite rightly insisted that poetry was by its nature subjective, went on to describe it as the medium through which man retires into his inner self, *thereby to regain communion with his fellows.*

The degree of privacy varies enormously. Spenser and Bunyan, for instance, are very different from each other; yet, when we set them against twentieth-century parabolists, they seem to draw closer together. In his book about the making of allegory, *Dark Conceit*, Edwin Honig finds that Kafka takes his place naturally in the ancient tradition. 'It is', he writes, 'as though the typical formula for the Christian hero, which Dante set up and Bunyan renewed, had been adapted by Kafka with all the old terms intact save the consolation of a supernatural grace.' The qualification is a very important one but Honig sees that with other modern authors much larger qualifications have to be made. 'Some explanation for the elusive pattern and the increasing ambiguity in modern allegories may be found in the destruction of the rigid base of cultural authority upon which allegory traditionally depended, and in the relatively greater stress put upon the autonomy of the artist since the Reformation.' But there are writers, such as Beckett and William Golding, where the pattern has become more elusive again and the ambiguities more frequent and complex than in any of the writers Mr Honig mentions. These are difficulties to be faced later. Let us get back to the comparatively firm ground of *The Faerie Queene* and *Pilgrim's Progress.*

In the last chapter after touching on the question of belief and then on the importance of shared experiences or attitudes, I suggested what may seem a somewhat naïve criterion, that of self-identification. In answer to Mr Esslin who found it a virtue in his playwrights of the Absurd that one cannot 'identify' with their characters, I maintained that it was one of their virtues that one very often can. And, when there is no one to identify with, I would suggest that the work is inferior or at least comparatively trivial, like some of Ionesco's plays. Mr Esslin is also an admirer of Brecht but I cannot accept the Brechtian principle of 'alienation'.

How far can one identify with the characters in Spenser and Bunyan? In *The Faerie Queene* I could not identify with either Sir Guyon, the Knight of Temperance, or Sir Artegall, the Knight of Justice, but I could with the hero of the first book, the Knight of the Red Cross. This is because, though this Knight is intended to represent Holiness, more often than not he is Everyman, searching for truth and finding it or losing it. I could also identify with Sir Calidore, the hero of book VI, who is one of the least allegorical knights, is more able to relax than most of them, and also appreciates poetry. Now, if all the knights were of the Guyon–Artegall type, *The Faerie Queene* would not be the great work it is. As for *Pilgrim's Progress*, provided he will forget his sectarian or anti-religious prejudices, anyone ought to be able to identify with Christian. For Christian is Everyman again, and his quest can stand for any quest that begins in anguish and ends in self-conquest and death; just as in modern literature Golding's Pincher Martin is Everyman and his struggle stands for any struggle that ends in death and defeat.

The medieval morality play called *Everyman* provides in fact an obvious prototype for Bunyan though not for Spenser. The structure of *Everyman* is an even better example of a strait and narrow path than *Pilgrim's Progress* itself. It moves forward inexorably from beginning to end and there are no ambiguities. And, although it is in verse, it is not in the obvious sense 'poetic', as are certain religious lyrics of about the same period, such as *Quia Amore Langueo*. Its virtues are the prose virtues of Bunyan, and its characters, though personifications of the simplest type, speak with the same tone of voice as characters in Bunyan such as Pliable. Pliable, when floundering in the Slough of Despond, says: 'May I get out again with my life, you shall possess the brave country alone for me.' Pliable is of the same breed as the prevaricating Fellowship in *Everyman* who, when asked to bear Everyman company on his dangerous journey, replies:

> That is matter indeed. Promise is duty;
> But, and I should take such a voyage on me,
> I know it well, it should be to my gain . . .

A little later Everyman reproaches him:

> Ye promised otherwise, pardie.

To which Fellowship, speaking now like Bunyan's Talkative, rejoins,

> I wot well I said so, truly:
> And yet if thou wilt eat, and drink, and make good cheer,
> Or haunt to women the lusty company,
> I would not forsake you while the day is clear,
> Trust me verily.

The style in *Everyman* is spare and undecorated and sometimes colloquial: such a style will recur in many forms of parable writing up to our own time. But usually it is only the style that is so straightforward. The general treatment

of the theme remains, to take Spenser's own phrase for
The Faerie Queene, a 'dark conceit'.

Everyman, like *Pilgrim's Progress* later, came from the
people and was addressed to them. A more sophisticated
writer in the fifteenth century, the Scottish poet Robert
Henryson, author of the frighteningly naturalistic 'Testament of Cresseid', was also capable of producing a thor-
oughly traditional kind of allegorical poem in 'The Bludy
Serk'. Here an aged King (he had been reigning sixty years)
has a beautiful daughter. A grotesquely ugly giant seizes
her and throws her into a dungeon. Her father sends out
looking for a champion; 'a worthy Prince that had no peir'
takes up the quest, overcomes the giant and casts him into
his own dungeon. But in the fight the knight has been
grievously wounded so that his sark, or shirt, is all bloody.
The lady laments on his behalf but he hands her the bloody
sark and asks her to hang it up to serve as a reminder to her
when men come to woo her. She does so. Having told the
story, Henryson takes the trouble to make the moral quite
clear—one, in fact, for him who runs to read. The King
represents the Trinity, the lady man's soul, the giant Lucifer,
and the Knight Christ. To us such an explicit *significatio*
may seem to take away from the story, or from the poetry:
we tend to feel, 'Oh the poetry's just there to sugar the pill,'
as if the poet had started with a naked message and then
coldbloodedly decided to dress it up in such and such a way.
But it seems unlikely that Henryson's mind worked like
that. For one thing, although he was dealing in allegorical
commonplaces, that does not mean that they would have
sounded frigid or rung empty in his time. On the contrary,
the representation of man's soul as a lady in distress was as

31

familiar in the Middle Ages as the fact that grass is green. We find it again, more lyrically and movingly, in *Quia Amore Langueo* where 'in the valley of restless mind' a bleeding man is sitting under a tree on a hill:

> I am treulove that fals was never;
> my sistur, mannys soul, I loved hyr thus . . .

Bunyan also used commonplaces, in his case often drawn from the Bible, especially the Pauline epistles—'the whole armour of God' and so on. Another Protestant writer of the seventeenth century, George Herbert, wrote many poems which, as Rosamond Tuve has shown exhaustively, are permeated with traditional symbols common in medieval services, hymns and iconography: the fact of the Reformation had not yet taken away from their efficacy.

Similarly, Spenser is full of traditional material: similarly and yet, of course, differently. It is not only that *The Faerie Queene* is complex where these other works are simple, and evasive or elusive where they are straightforward. It is, more basically, that where *Everyman* and the medieval devotional lyrics and *Pilgrim's Progress* are specifically Christian works, *The Faerie Queene*, for all Spenser's Christianity, is only so incidentally. Mr Honig writes that *The Faerie Queene* 'is a poem that justifies not the ways of God to man but the ways of man to man'. We need not of course fully trust Spenser's own account of his poem in the letter to Raleigh, but when he writes that 'the generall end of all the book is to fashion a gentleman or noble person in vertuous and gentle discipline', it does at least indicate that we are in a different mental world from that of *Everyman* earlier or *Pilgrim's Progress* later. Spenser was admittedly an enthusiastic

Protestant, not to say a bitter anti-Papist, yet, as Mr Hough has pointed out, he has very much in common with Tasso, the poet of the Counter-Reformation. We could say, I think, that he is more basically Christian than he is Protestant; we could also say that *The Faerie Queene*, though concerned most of the time with morals, is not primarily a religious work, let alone a mystical one. Compare, for example, Despair in the first book of *The Faerie Queene* with Bunyan's Giant Despair. It is not only that the latter is a great blustering oaf and the former a crafty rhetorician whose

> subtle tongue, like dropping honny, mealt'th
> Into the hart, and searcheth every vaine . . .

A more important difference is that Giant Despair is simply and solely the enemy of Christian's *faith* whereas what the Red Cross Knight is being tempted to is the medieval deadly sin of accidie; this was not only a prevalent medieval temptation but also a very common Elizabethan one. Both Hamlet and the Red Cross Knight are drawn towards suicide; in neither case is the argument primarily a Christian one.

I have already mentioned what I called 'double-level writing' or 'sleight-of-hand writing'. In the simplest form of allegory there is none of this: it is all a matter of one-for-one correspondences: it is no more double-level than algebra. But Spenser, as has been known from his own day, can run various different kinds of allegory—e.g. the moral and the historical—simultaneously. Modern criticism has analysed and emphasized the very great variety in Spenser —not only the variety of the ground covered, which ranges from the dangers of accidie to the delights of pastoral, and from the psychology of love to the problems of Time and Eternity, but also the varieties of his approach or, as we might say, the way he keeps changing his camera angles. Graham Hough, examining *The Faerie Queene* in the light of Freud's theory of dreams, finds it full of instances of what Freud called 'condensation'—the construction 'of collective and composite personages'. For this reason, writes Mr Hough, 'an element of ambiguity is an essential part of his [Spenser's] imaginative procedure'. This is one reason why Spenser seems to have a special relevance for us today.

As Mr Hough points out, Spenser also illustrates another Freudian dream-process which is the converse of condensation: 'an individual dream-thought may be represented by several different elements in the dream-content'. Hough gives as example the figures of Amoret, Belphoebe and Florimell where an original bud or cell has broken, so to speak, into three. Both these processes are often to be found in modern drama and the modern novel. What we do not meet today—or at least it is very rare—is the sort of trick vision you find here and there in *The Faerie Queene* and notably in Spenser's *Prothalamion*. In Spenser's time and for some time before him, though not for so long after, there was nothing odd about such a way of presenting things; but the fact that a modern reader can read the *Prothalamion* without finding it odd is simply a tribute to Spenser's genius. For what happens in this very peculiar poem? First we have an obviously genuine personal note: Spenser walks out to ease his pain 'along the shoare of silver streaming Themmes'. At once he runs into a flock of nymphs 'with goodly greenish locks' gathering flowers in little wicker baskets: the modern reader can accept this quite easily

because it is in the familiar neo-classical pastoral convention, just as he can accept similar oddities in *Lycidas*. In
the third stanza we meet two swans—introduced to us
simply as swans, though they are exceptionally white. These
swans proceed down stream, admired by the nymphs who
throw flowers at them and followed by all the wild fowl on
the river. And you know the rest of the story. 'At length
they all to mery London came' where, next door to the
Temple, two noble bridegrooms are waiting—these 'gentle
Knights' are introduced to us as human. But where are the
brides? They are the swans. Spenser does not bother to
contrive a metamorphosis.

> These two forth pacing to the Rivers side,
> Received those two faire Brides, their Loves delight—

and that is that. It is all perfectly acceptable, and meaningful.

We meet the same sort of vision—and the same method
—in *The Faerie Queene*. I give no examples of Spenser's use
of Graeco-Roman myth (with which he was as familiar as
Bunyan was with the Bible) but will only mention that he
used figures such as Venus and Diana for very much more
than decoration: they are dynamic principles and three-
dimensional—contrast the comparatively two-dimensional
writing of Tennyson in, say, that fine poem 'Tithonus'.
Spenser's other figures range from the crudest kind of
personified abstraction to a character like Britomart who
contrives to be both allegorical and human, and to figures
who are not allegorical at all. Here are two examples of
blatant allegory: the first I can accept, the second not. The
first, from book IV, canto V, is the cottage of Care where Sir
Scudamour has to put up for the night. It is a little cottage

but it contains Care himself and six assistants. Care is a hollow-eyed, smoke-blackened, blistered creature—

> a blacksmith by his trade,
> That neither day nor night from working spared,
> But to small purpose yron wedges made:
> Those be unquiet thoughts, that carefull minds invade.

The racket of their hammering keeps the lovelorn Sir Scudamour awake and, when he does drop off, the master smith nips him in the side with a pair of red-hot tongs.

This is crude, but it makes an effective cartoon. I cannot, however, accept my second example, the figure of Ate in the first canto of the same fourth book. Ate, as her name shows, is first and last a trouble-maker. I cannot accept her because I cannot envisage her. Spenser represents her as having ears that don't match, feet that don't match and so on, which is all very well as idea—or rhetorical device of the sort the Romans were so fond of—but will not work as picture.

> And as her eares so eke her feet were odde,
> And much unlike, th'one long, the other short,
> And both misplast; that when th'one forward yode,
> The other back retired, and contrarie trode.

I find it a relief to turn to a really palpable monster such as the Savage Man who in book IV, canto VII, carries off Amoret.

> His neather lip was not like man nor beast,
> But like a wide deepe poke, downe hanging low,
> In which he wont the relickes of his feast,
> And cruell spoyle, which he had spard, to stow:
> And over it his huge great nose did grow,
> Full dreadfully empurpled all with bloud;
> And downe both sides two wide long eares did glow,
> And raught down to his waste, when up he stood,
> More great than th'eares of Elephants by Indus flood.

This Savage Man is grotesque enough but in a quite different way from Ate. He would have the entrée to nursery horror stories and Elizabethan travellers' tales and bestiaries; Ate would not.

Now let us sample a very different passage of *The Faerie Queene*, which is allegorical, though not obtrusively so, and at the same time has the haunting quality of a dream; this means that its physical weight is at least equal to its mental weight. A great deal, understandably, has been written about the Bower of Bliss in the last canto of the second book, but critics have tended to skip over what is the last lap on the way to that goal. Spenser himself does not skip over it but gives it nearly forty stanzas. Here the Knight of Temperance, attended by his indefatigable Palmer and one professional boatman, is sailing over allegorical seas which are also seas of dream. We may remember, without making too much of it, the importance psychologists attach to dreams of water; we may also remember De Quincey's alarming dreams of endless oceans where innumerable human faces are superimposed upon the waves. In Spenser on the third day 'an hideous roaring farre away they heard', and the boat has to make its way between the Gulf of Greediness (an allegorical variant of Charybdis) and the Rock of Vile Reproach (a variant of Scylla). The language here—as is usual when Spenser means business—is taut and straightforward:

> Forthy, this hight *The Rocke of* vile *Reproch*,
>   A daungerous and detestable place,
>   To which nor fish nor fowle did once approch,
>   But yelling Meawes, with Seagulles hoarse and bace,
>   And Cormoyrants, with birds of ravenous race,

> Which still sate waiting on that wastefull clift,
> For spoyle of wretches, whose unhappie cace,
> After lost credite and consumed thrift,
> At last them driven hath to this despairefull drift.

Having passed between these two dangers they come to another archetypal image, the insidious Wandering Islands where, true to dream behaviour (and one can compare fairy stories and Lewis Carroll's Alice books), a character left behind six cantos earlier reappears to pursue them in a little skippet. This is 'the wanton Phaedria', the lady of the Idle Lake, who symbolizes 'Immodest Mirth'. She is not a serious menace and the Palmer easily makes her turn her boat about by moralizing at her. Next comes another 'narrow way' between the Quicksand of Unthriftyhed and the Whirlpool of Decay. Once again the allegory satisfies the head while the physical details—e.g. the checked and discoloured wave over the quicksand—supply the dream dimension that engages the rest of the reader. Next comes a fine parade of sea monsters:

> All dreadfull pourtraicts of deformitee:
> Spring-headed Hydraes, and sea-shouldring Whales—

and, after them, a temptation of the same type but much more powerful than Phaedria—the Mermaids, imitated from the sirens in the *Odyssey* but transmuted:

> O thou fair sonne of gentle Faery,
> That art in mighty armes most magnifide
> Above all knights, that ever battell tride,
> O turne thy rudder hither-ward a while:
> Here may thy storme-bet vessell safely ride;
> This is the Port of rest from troublous toyle,
> The world's sweet In, from paine and wearisome turmoyle.

(The last line is a good example of how Spenser can use the often boring Alexandrine for a deliberate rallentando, a functional effect of languor.) We are now getting near the land which contains the Bower of Bliss, but, just as the beguiling Phaedria was sandwiched between two nastinesses, Spenser here sandwiches a real little piece of nightmare between the blissful land and the beguiling mermaids. The boat is enveloped in a sudden 'grosse fog', and

> Suddeinly an innumerable flight
> Of harmefull birds about them fluttering, cride,
> And with their wicked wings them oft did smight,
> And sore annoyed, groping in that griesly night.

Anyone who, like myself, hates being cooped up in a room, let alone a dark room, with a bird that keeps flying round wildly, will agree that this is an apt last item in this dream sequence.

A more famous passage, this time of complicated allegory but which also has the strength of dream, is the house of the enchanter Busirane in which Amoret is kept prisoner and tortured. Here an outer room of tapestries leads into an inner room of pure gold from which an iron door leads into an empty third room where Amoret is fastened to a brazen pillar. It is perhaps worth noticing that Freud wrote in *The Interpretation of Dreams:* 'The dream of walking through a row of rooms is a brothel or harem dream.' This fits in with the likely interpretation of this episode. Before leaving this dream aspect of Spenser I should like to refer to the suggestive comparison that Dr Janet Spens makes between the girl with the pitcher in Wordsworth's *Prelude*, set in a landscape of 'visionary dreariness', and the girl with the pitcher seen by Una in *The Faerie Queene*.

So much for the Spenser of the dreams. Lastly, let us glance at the Spenser of the humours—both in the ordinary sense and in the Ben Jonson sense. Spenser's more comic characters such as Braggadochio, Trompart and Malbecco are forerunners of Ben Jonson's knaves and fools. Canto X of book III is indeed a canto of Humours. Paridell, like Volpone, is a type rather than a character, and is—until he achieves it—dedicated to the seduction of Hellenore, the beautiful wife of Malbecco, a repulsive one-eyed old miser:

> So perfect in that art was *Paridell*,
> That he Malbeccoes halfen eye did wyle,
> His halfen eye he wiled wondrous well . . .

Hellenore is only too willing to be seduced and, like any scheming woman in the Comedy of Humours, thinks up a cleft-stick device for defeating her husband. Having looted his treasury she sets the rest on fire.

> This second Hellene, faire Dame Hellenore,
> The whiles her husband ranne with sory haste,
> To quence the flames, which she had tyn'd before,
> Laught at his foolish labour spent in waste;
> And ranne into her lovers armes right fast;
> Where streight embraced, she to him did cry,
> And call aloud for helpe, ere helpe were past;
> For loe that Guest would beare her forcibly,
> And meant to ravish her, that rather had to dy.

Malbecco dithers to and fro between his burning goods and his abducted wife and loses them both. During the rest of the Canto Spenser piles up his discomfiture. Meanwhile Paridell, having got what he wants from Hellenore, forsakes her. It is as ruthless as anything in Jonson, but as this action takes place in Faerie Land Spenser can go further. Hellenore, abandoned by her lover, goes to live promiscuously with a troop of satyrs—and enjoys it. Malbecco spies on her as a satyr makes love to her, later asks her to return to him, and is rejected. The satyrs chase him away, butting him with their horns, he escapes and looks for the last of his treasure, only to find it has been stolen from its hiding place by the deplorable character Trompart. Now at last he becomes mad and throws himself down from a cliff, only to find that he is so wasted away that he cannot kill himself by falling. His madness—which could not happen in Jonson—now becomes a sort of apotheosis. Here is an instance in Spenser where a character ends more allegorical than he began. In the last stanza of the Canto Malbecco is left in a cave, feeding on toads and frogs:

> Yet can he never dye, but dying lives,
> And doth himselfe with sorrow new sustaine,
> That death and life attonce unto him gives,
> And painefull pleasure turnes to pleasing paine.
> There dwels he ever, miserable swaine,
> Hatefull both to him selfe, and every wight;
> Where he through privy griefe, and horrour vaine,
> Is woxen so deform'd, that he has quight
> Forgot he was a man, and Gealosie is hight.

Edwin Honig in *Dark Conceit* notes that 'criticism usually puts satire opposite to allegory'; he considers this a mistake. In the twentieth century certainly we often find satire intertwined with something that is very like allegory. The story of Malbecco shows that Spenser also on occasions did a similar intertwining. It is from this side of Spenser, the Spenser of the Humours, that we can conveniently move on to Bunyan. Was not Bunyan, for one thing, always inventing characters such as Mr By-ends from the town of Fair-speech: 'and to tell you the truth, I am become a gentleman of good quality, yet my great-grandfather was but a waterman, looking one way and rowing another, and I got most of my estate by the same occupation'? Or, from *The Holy War*, there is Mr Pitiless's speech from the dock when he pleads: 'Not guilty of pitilessness: all I did was to "cheer up", according to my name, for my name is not *Pitiless*, but *Cheer-up*; and I could not abide to see Mansoul inclined to melancholy.' Then there is the broad humour of Diabolus's letters from the pit, ending for instance: 'From our dreadful confines in the most fearful pit, we salute you, and so do those many legions here with us, wishing you may be as hellishly prosperous as we desire to be ourselves.' The logic in all this, the predetermined behaviour 'in character', is not only reminiscent of Ben Jonson; it also anticipates *Gulliver*.

Here a few dates may be helpful. The first three books of *The Faerie Queene* were published in 1590. *Volpone* was brought out in 1605. George Herbert, the poet who stands nearest to Bunyan, died in 1632, when Bunyan was hardly four. Bunyan himself was in Bedford gaol from 1660 to 1672; the Restoration had taken place shortly before. The first part of *Pilgrim's Progress* was published in 1678. During this period of less than a century enormous changes took place in England. *The Faerie Queene*, as has often been remarked, was already out of date when it was published. For all that, as C. S. Lewis puts it, Spenser remains 'the great mediator between the Middle Ages and the modern poets, the man who saved us from the catastrophe of too thorough a renaissance'. As for Bunyan, at the end of the period he was no more in danger of that particular catastrophe than he was of catching the late seventeenth-century

Enlightenment. Nor was he put out of date by the Restoration. Where Spenser had been a gentleman writing for gentlemen, Bunyan was of the people and wrote for the people—and from now on Puritanism was something not to be dislodged from the English popular heritage. But like Spenser he retains his medieval elements. Scholars like Dr Janet Spens and Professor Lewis have pointed out one common source for Spenser and Bunyan—'the old-fashioned sermon in the village church still continuing the allegorical tradition of the medieval pulpit'. As Lewis says, 'We have long looked for the origins of *The Faerie Queene* in Renaissance palaces and Platonic academies, and forgotten that it has humbler origins of at least equal importance in the Lord Mayor's show, the chap-book, the bedtime story, the family Bible, and the village church.' So has *Pilgrim's Progress*; and Professor Lewis's next remark applies equally to Bunyan: 'What lies next beneath the surface in Spenser's poem is the world of popular imagination'—and below that again 'the primitive or instinctive mind, with all its terrors and ecstasies'.

So much for the common background of Spenser and Bunyan—and also for their very great differences in background. If we now compare *The Faerie Queene* and *Pilgrim's Progress* themselves, the first thing we notice is their completely different construction and geography. *The Faerie Queene* could not possibly be mapped, and mapping *Pilgrim's Progress* would be like mapping the Nile valley, only worse. All longitude and practically no latitude: that is the trouble with a strait and narrow path and it is only the ups and downs which keep it dramatically interesting, the Hill Difficulty, the Valley of Humiliation, the Valley of the

Shadow of Death, the Delectable Mountains. There is also of course always the menace from the forbidden country on each side—like the unknown menaces off stage in a play by Harold Pinter. Still, as regards story the fact remains that Spenser's is highly complicated, a cluster of stories something like a banyan tree, while Bunyan's is simple and relentlessly straightforward—more like a pine tree. At the same time, in *Pilgrim's Progress* there *is* an incipient Chinese-box arrangement. The whole thing is put forward as a dream of Bunyan's: this dream contains the main allegory of Christian's, and later Christiana's, journey, and in each of these again a very important episode is the visit to the Interpreter's House which is the occasion for allegories within the allegory.

The dream device is one that normally irritates me but in this case I do not object to it since from the very start it involves Bunyan personally: for it is he who is watching Christian—who after all is not only Everyman but also Bunyan himself. I am not so happy, however, about the Interpreter's House. Off the road and out of the open air, I find that here we are back too obviously near the pulpit: there is a rustle of sermon notes, the moral charades are too calculated. Thus in part i I can accept the 'very large parlour that was full of dust' which signifies 'the heart of a man that was never sanctified by the sweet grace of the gospel', but I baulk at the next example of the two little children Passion and Patience, mainly, I think, because of the time problem involved: Christian is only having a quick look round but, while he watches, the spendthrift boy Passion has to demand and get hold of a fortune, lavish it all away and reduce himself to rags. But I may be suffering

44

here from period prejudice, as perhaps I was with Spenser's Ate. After all, if the Interpreter were around today he could show us the fortunes of Passion just as quickly as this on a screen: we can all accept it when the ciné-camera speeds up the life of a plant. All the same this is not one of the more vivid charades or tableaux. What one does remember from the Interpreter's House in part I is the man in the iron cage; and in part II the man with the muck-rake.

These moral spectacles laid on by the Interpreter draw on the same type of imagery as the parables of Jesus. They can also remind us of the poems of George Herbert, who anticipates Bunyan not only in his household and everyday images but also in the plainness of his diction. To return to the comparison of Bunyan and Spenser, we have noticed in *The Faerie Queene* the constantly shifting ratio between allegory and non-allegorical elements, such as romance for its own sake. Some of Spenser's figures, such as the shepherds in book VI, are not allegorical at all. Bunyan has none of this variety. His material is *all* sermon material. Why then does his story so haunt us in an age when sermons are considered unreadable? The answer, I suggest, is sleight-of-hand but this time, probably, used unconsciously. Moreover, compared with modern writers like Pinter, Bunyan's sleight-of-hand works the other way round. Pinter gives us what would pass for a dramatized slice of life and slips in between the lines, so to speak, his recurrent theme of a cosmic menace. Bunyan starts with his overt theme—which is the orthodox Puritan gospel—but, thanks to his own intense experience and also his acute observation, the pulpit abstractions become concrete and speak with the voice of human beings. This is his great achievement.

This brings me to the question of technique. Spenser was a Cambridge scholar and knew his classics and his Ariosto. But Bunyan, apart from the Bible, was not influenced by literature. The Bible certainly was an important influence but, as regards sheer style, even more important was the spoken word: he must have been a very good listener. Here again, before we dismiss Spenser, let us make one more comparison, allowing for the basic difference between prose and verse. The few quotations I have made from Spenser should at least suggest that, in spite of his very artificial stanza and his monotonous and tiresome archaisms, he is not for the most part 'poetic' in the narrow and derogatory sense. Far from his lines being languorous and sugary, they are much more often what the later Yeats wanted *his* lines to be—'athletic'. Compared with Shelley and Keats he is a bony and sinewy poet. Mr Eliot said once that good verse should show the virtues of good prose. Spenser can be prosy in the bad sense but he far more frequently reveals what Mr Eliot was asking for:

> The donghill kind
> Delights in filth and foule incontinence:
> Let *Grill* be *Grill*, and have his hoggish mind . . .

The same prose virtues reappear in George Herbert, who uses the same sort of 'extended metaphor' to which the Elizabethan rhetoric books gave the name of allegory. Thus time changes from an executioner into a gardener:

> An usher to convey our souls
> Beyond the utmost starres and poles.

The first of Herbert's two poems on Prayer, a sonnet without a single indicative verb, consists of a breathless accumulation of metaphorical images of different kinds, most of which would be too paradoxical for Bunyan; in between these paradoxes, however, Herbert slips in suggestive simplicities:

> A kind of tune, which all things heare and fear,

while his 'land of spices' belongs to the same landscape as the Delectable Mountains and Bunyan's Land of Beulah. Some of Herbert's poems are open, orthodox, allegorical narratives which link him with both Spenser and Bunyan. Such is 'The Pilgrimage':

> The gloomy cave of Desperation
> I left on th'one, and on the other side
> The rock of Pride—

and so on through 'Fancies medow', 'Cares cops', and 'the wilde of Passion'. And sometimes this staid Anglican clergyman, if only in his phrasing, approached the territory of Humours:

> Then came brave Glorie *puffing* by
> In silks that *whistled* . . .

The italics are mine. My main point here is that Herbert, though writing in verse, is not only less strained or straining than the other so-called Metaphysical poets, but a good deal less 'poetical' than certain prose writers of the period such as Jeremy Taylor and Sir Thomas Browne.

Bunyan is equally unostentatious—and equally effective. If Herbert's verse, like much of Spenser's, has the virtues of prose, Bunyan's prose has the virtues of good conversation. And I do not mean only in his excellent dialogue. Like a crafty talker, or actor, Bunyan is a master of the quiet aside and the conspicuous throw-away. Here are two examples of what he can do with a parenthesis. First, from the 'gentleman-like' Demas who tries to get pilgrims off the road to see the silver mine. When asked if it isn't dangerous, he replies: 'Not very dangerous except to those that are careless (but withal, he blushed as he spoke).' The second comes from Giant Despair when he loses his temper with Christian and Hopeful because they refuse to commit suicide. 'With that he looked ugly upon them, and, rushing to them, had doubtless made an end of them himself, but that he fell into one of his fits (for he sometimes, in sunshiny weather, fell into fits), and lost for a time the use of his hand.' There is a beautiful irony, which Bunyan in no way presses, in that phrase 'in sunshiny weather'.

I mention these points of style not so much for their own sake as because in Bunyan, as in some modern parabolists, there is a more fundamental irony in the contrast between their matter-of-fact or earthy or everyday mode of expression and their cosmic or mystical themes. Donne's sermons can terrify but I doubt whether those 'terrors and ecstasies', ascribed by Professor Lewis to the 'popular imagination'— and they seem even more dominant in the Puritan imagination—are not more hauntingly conveyed by Bunyan's understated prose with its naturally subtle rhythms. The popular Puritan imagination still expresses itself in a similar way. In 1944 a book was published called *The Lady of the Hare*, described as 'a study in the healing power of dreams'. In the first half of this book its author, John Layard, a Jungian psychologist, recounts a series of interviews which he had with a very devout working-class woman from Northern Ireland. In one of these interviews the woman describes how recently she had a 'wonderful experience'. 'She went to bed at the usual time, but woke up with a feeling of things rushing to and fro in her head, with the result that her head was "like to burst". This went on for a long time, with a feeling that something was sawing backwards and forwards in her brain, and every time it sawed a voice said, "O Jesus, I have promised . . ." As she lay suffering in this way in her head, the voice repeated itself with even greater intensity, till she heard the clock striking twelve . . . when suddenly she herself started to repeat the words, altered into "Jesus, I renew my promise"; and then with a feeling of intense relief fell off to sleep.' This surely is very much the world of Bunyan's Christian.

One last example of Bunyan's prose which, among other things, shows him quite naturally introducing a recent invention, the telescope. More significantly, the pilgrims here, as so often in Bunyan and like so many other heroes in parable writing, are shown in a state of doubtful suspension: they have to persuade themselves that the white whale still exists or that Godot will come in the end. Christian and Hopeful are on the Delectable Mountains. 'Then said the Shepherds one to another, Let us here show to the pilgrims the gates of the Celestial City, if they have skill to look through our perspective glass. The pilgrims then lovingly accepted the notion; so they had them to the top of a high hill, called Clear, and gave them their glass to look. Then they essayed to look, but the remembrance of that last thing that the Shepherds had shown them [the by-way to hell] made their hands shake; by means of which impediment, they could not look steadily through the glass; yet they thought they saw something like the gate, and also some of the glory of the place.'

This kind of primitive Christian imagination survives today, but though it may get into psychiatrists' casebooks, its day in literature is past; and indeed has been past a long time. In the next chapter I shall discuss the Romantic Revival and its aftermath. This means that I shall have crossed the Great Divide which separates us not only from Spenser but from the Shakespeare who wrote 'The Phoenix and the Turtle' and from poets like Donne and Herbert. Rosamond Tuve has written that 'metaphysical wit and concord of unlikes in an image is precisely the operation, much condensed, of the old (and maligned) allegorical mode of writing'. When we have crossed the Great Divide, I shall prefer not to talk of allegory but of parable, using it in the wide sense I gave it at the outset. For such allegories as do appear will be, unlike *The Faerie Queene* and *Pilgrim's Progress*, drifting rather than anchored. And never again will a poet of George Herbert's calibre be able quite naturally to express his feelings about Redemption in an out-and-out allegorical sonnet in everyday diction and with images drawn from something so prosaic as real estate (Hounds of Heaven are another matter).

> Having been tenant long to a rich Lord,
>   Not thriving, I resolved to be bold,
>   And make a suit unto him, to afford
> A new small-rented lease and cancell th'old.
> In heaven at his manour I him sought:
>   They told me there that he was lately gone
>   About some land, which he had dearly bought
> Long since on earth, to take possession.
> I straight return'd, and knowing his great birth,
>   Sought him accordingly in great resorts;
>   In cities, theatres, gardens, parks, and courts:
> At length I heard a ragged noise and mirth
>   Of theeves and murderers: there I him espied,
>   Who straight, *Your suit is granted*, said, and died.

III

THE ROMANTICS

WHEN I said that no English poet after his time would be able to write again like George Herbert, I did not of course mean that there could be no later poet holding Herbert's beliefs and equally impelled to express them in poetry. But in a poet belief cannot be disentangled from other things, from his personal experience and attitude. Again, his personal experience and attitude do not exist in a vacuum but are conditioned by time and place, by the general experience and attitude of the community in which he finds himself. And if he revolts against that communal experience and attitude, he is still being none the less conditioned by it. These are all truisms but they need repeating in order to explain why I am writing about the poets of the Romantic Revival. I should have liked to entitle this book 'From Spenser to Beckett'; on the surface it would have seemed feasible to jump right on from the mid-seventeenth century to the mid-nineteenth or even the late nineteenth. But I felt I could not do this. By bringing in a poet like Shelley I run the risk of clouding the issue, of cramming too many dissimilar kinds of writing into an inadequate receptacle or, if you prefer, of hopelessly mixing my drinks. But to leave him out in this context would be, I think, dishonest; it would be like suppressing a bend sinister in one's family tree, an extremely important bend sinister. For, whether we like it or not, an English writer of the twentieth century must have much more of

Shelley in him than of Spenser, say, or Herbert or Bunyan. Mr Eliot's famous lament about the dissociation of sensibility at the end of the seventeenth century got a sympathetic hearing in this country, but with the best will in the world the sympathetic hearers could not put their own sensibilities together again. Certainly between the two world wars younger poets turned back to the Metaphysicals and imitated something of their technique, but such imitations were of the surface. Over the gulf that lies between us no one can imitate an attitude. As for Mr Eliot himself, whatever his preaching, in his practice he could not escape his heritage—or recover his lost heritage. In spite of himself his poetry fails to be impersonal—and it is not classical either. 'Why should the aged eagle stretch its wings?' *The Waste Land* is nearer in feeling to Shelley's *The Triumph of Life* than it is to anything before the French Revolution or the Industrial Revolution.

But why should I include these Romantic poets in a survey of parable writing? The first obvious answer is negative: because they are not realists, and do not attempt to be objective. Even when they appear to be describing things, a landscape for instance, this is not what they are doing primarily. Thus Coleridge confesses that 'in looking at objects of Nature' he is looking rather for 'a symbolical language for something within me that already and forever exists, than observing anything new'. I have already quoted the statement of C. S. Lewis that allegory came 'to supply the *subjective* element in literature'. But I have also referred to the distinction so often drawn by poets themselves and by critics between 'allegory', which they usually despise, and 'symbolism', which they usually extol.

Coleridge himself draws this distinction very strongly, even though—to look again at the poet's practice—it would be hard to argue that *The Ancient Mariner* is completely free of allegorical elements. The same distinction is made by W. H. Auden and Norman Holmes Pearson in their Introduction to the fourth volume of their huge anthology, *Poets of the English Language*. Assuming that an allegorical image means a one-to-one correspondence, they regard a 'symbol' by contrast as something essentially ambiguous: 'To the question "What does it symbolize?" only multiple and equally partial answers are possible.' I think myself that they carry this too far. For example, they go on to write: 'We may say, if we like, that the sun and the moon in *The Ancient Mariner* symbolize respectively the punishing justice-demanding Father and the forgiving merciful Mother; we are not wrong but we are very little nearer understanding the poem, for a hundred equally valid allegorical identifications can be made.' A hundred? Surely not a hundred? Anyhow, whatever the sun and moon may represent in it, surely the gist of *The Ancient Mariner* is something most people would agree about; the main story seems almost as inevitable as the adventures of the Third Son in a typical folk tale, though these also include apparently arbitrary elements. Auden and Pearson point out that, while there is an allegorical method, 'there can be no method of symbolism'. But they rightly add the qualification that 'in nearly all successful allegory the images used do in fact have a symbolic value over and above their allegorical use'. This is exactly the same concession that Blake made when he allowed that *Pilgrim's Progress*, though an allegory (which for Blake was an 'inferior kind of poetry'), was also full of Vision or Imagination, by which he meant 'a Representation of what Eternally Exists, Really and Unchangeably'.

But, though it is not so usually admitted, the converse would seem also to be true. In most successful symbolical writing, such as *The Ancient Mariner*, there tends to be a hard core or rather a spine of allegory. The spine may be buried deep but it holds the poem up. And we should not be misled by the recurrent phrase 'one-to-one correspondence'. We have seen that in *The Faerie Queene* itself there are often multiple correspondences. So there are in *Waiting for Godot*. The ratio between 'allegory' and 'symbolism' is obviously not the same in these two works but both elements are present. Suppose there is an idea A that is to be allegorized. Let us call the allegorical image for it x. Then you cannot complain, unless you want to be confined to very naïve allegory indeed, if you more often meet the image in the form of xy or xyz and so on; or the other way round, if the one image x sometimes stands for ideas A *plus B*. Such blends and such pluses are today more frequent than ever. The modern writer, the more suspicious he becomes of a spurious objectivity or realism, is the more impelled to the projection of special worlds. This is nothing new but there are different ways of making them. Spenser made his in one way, Shelley in quite another. Certain modern writers, though they have ways of their own, are at moments comparable to Spenser and at others to Shelley. Which is the point of this preamble.

When I was seventeen two of my favourite longer poems were Blake's *Book of Thel* and Shelley's *Prometheus Unbound*. These are very different from each other, although

54

when viewed in a historical perspective they appear to draw close together. Today I can still read *The Book of Thel* with pleasure but for decades I have been most reluctant even to open *Prometheus*. A glance—even a very hurried and inadequate glance—at these two poems will at least raise some questions relevant to writing today. Blake is a freak phenomenon and can hardly be fitted into any critical framework. This, however, far from deterring the critics, has recently seemed to stimulate them. Thus Miss Kathleen Raine is very fond of applying the word 'archetypal' to Blake; she writes for instance that in Blake's early poems 'his roses and lambs are more than metaphorical, they are archetypal'. And this she relates to a theory of double-level or stratified symbolism which postulates that in all the greatest poetry there is 'an upper, linguistic layer, whose symbolic counters are words', and 'a lower, symbolic layer... that has little to do with words at all'. This reminds me that Esslin in *The Theatre of the Absurd* makes it a differentia of his playwrights that they deal in the Ineffable. In both cases my first reaction to such statements is to feel very uncomfortable. Is it proper, I ask myself, for a writer to concern himself with something that has little to do with words at all? But here we confront one of the eternal paradoxes: man wants to express himself because he cannot express himself—and this we meet in its most naked form in some contemporary writing. Both Miss Raine and Mr Esslin look for backing to modern psychology. 'The unconscious', writes Miss Raine, 'is innocent of words, but it formulates its desires and fears, its primordial but profound statements of living experience, in those symbolic forms that haunt our dreams.'

In discussing *The Faerie Queene* I have already agreed

55

with Mr Hough that the figures in Spenser tend to seem familiar because they have the quality of dream figures. But when we try to pin down the *symbolism* of dream figures we run two opposite risks, partly in accordance with which psychologists we read: either a particular image, say climbing a staircase, may be given a monotonously rigid and usually sexual significance, or so many allowances have to be made for each individual's peculiar mental make-up that any common factor may disappear entirely and one will be left with a bundle of images which are incomprehensible apart from that make-up. In Blake, for instance, Miss Raine perceives 'archetypes' (apparently in the Jungian sense) which come from Blake's unconscious. But she also insists that, when he was writing *The Book of Thel* and 'The Little Girl Lost' and 'The Little Girl Found', he was very much influenced by a recent translation by Thomas Taylor of Porphyry's *Cave of the Nymphs*. And she also, like other scholars, admits the enormous influence upon Blake of the Bible: in general, she is at pains to emphasize that 'Blake did not rely upon his own invention, but adapted traditional material'. This is so, but he adapted it in very strange ways. Miss Raine says that 're-naming and re-clothing the gods is one of the tasks of the makers of culture'. How much novelty or oddity in names or customs any particular reader can take depends upon both his imagination and his stamina.

Miss Raine, then, maintains very plausibly that *The Book of Thel* is 'based upon Porphyry's theme of the descent of the feminine soul into generation'. But an American scholar, Mr S. Foster Damon, who admits that this poem 'has usually been interpreted' in Miss Raine's way 'as the soul's refusal to leave Eternity and descend into this world

of generation', prefers himself to think of it as 'a recon-
sideration of the idea on which *Comus* is based.... Thel is
also the girl on the verge of womanhood, about to pass from
Innocence into Experience ... she questions successively
the meaning of her own innocence (the Lily), of the male
(the youthful Cloud), and of motherhood (the matron Clay
with her baby Worm).' 'Thel's flight back to innocence',
he concludes, 'seems to me to be simply the girl's natural
revulsion against the demands of her maturing flesh.' This
seems very different from the other interpretation; but Mr
Damon is prepared to admit—or rather claim—that *both*
could be true on the ground that 'the larger and smaller
patterns repeat each other'. I find this broadmindedness
worrying and rather reminiscent of the doctrine fashionable
in the 1920's that a poem can mean whatever meaning you
can find in it: probably under the influence of modern
psychology, some poets were themselves at that time only
too willing that their own works should be thus thought of
as free-for-all symbolical bran-tubs.

So I turn back to *The Book of Thel* and try to remember
what I found in it in my teens. A strong dream quality
certainly, established in the very first line:

The daughters of the Seraphim led round their sunny flocks

and an imagery which is fairly easy, being mostly traditional:

Ah! Thel is like a wat'ry bow, and like a parting cloud;
Like a reflection in a glass; like shadows in the water,
Like dreams of infants, like a smile upon an infant's face,
Like the dove's voice, like transient day, like music in the air.

Thirdly, a handling of rhythm which seemed perfectly
appropriate to the dream material. In the later Prophetic

Books the long lines tend to stick; in *The Book of Thel* they flow naturally. They are, apart from the last of the four sections, comparatively regular, seven stresses per line falling in a speakable fashion, yet with enough variety not to become jogtrot. Contrast

> Thy breath does nourish the innocent lamb; he smells thy
>   milky garments

with

> Art thou a Worm? image of weakness, art thou but a worm?

and again with

> The eternal gates' terrific porter lifted the northern bar.

So far so good. As far as detail is concerned, this poem struck me then very much as it strikes me now. But for me as a boy what did it all add up to? Certainly not to a neo-Platonist parable about the descent of the soul into the sphere of generation. On the contrary, at the very beginning of the poem, I took the lines

>   She in paleness sought the secret air,
> To fade away like morning beauty from her mortal day,

to imply that Thel was already *involved* in her mortal day, i.e. that the descent of the soul had already taken place. And when, immediately after this, Thel asks 'Why fade these children of the Spring, born but to smile and fall?' I assumed without questioning that these children of the spring were creatures on the plane of Time, not on the plane of Eternity. I had not yet heard of the neo-Platonist interpretation and the lines did not suggest it to me. Nor did they suggest Mr Foster Damon's interpretation. Reading the poem without any knowledge of Blake's esoteric cosmology, I was not at all conscious of what Mr

Damon calls 'Thel's natural revulsion against the demands of her maturing flesh'. Thus for Mr Damon the Clod of Clay represents motherhood but I took it quite literally when Thel says to the Clay:

And I complain'd in the mild air, because I fade away,
And lay me down in thy cold bed, and leave my shining lot.

I thought she was talking about the clay of the grave. Even more so, in the next section where Thel comes 'to her own graveplot', I assumed that this meant her own graveplot, not a Platonic incarceration in a sōma-sēma—the fleshly body which is the tomb of the spirit.

Now, if I were working on the 1920's principle of Gather Ye Symbols where Ye May, I suppose I could go one better than Mr Foster Damon and claim that, while both his interpretation and the neo-Platonist one were true, my teenage one (which remains my instinctive one) was equally true and all three of them could somehow coalesce. But I am reluctant to claim this because, even if it is true that in the other two 'the larger and smaller patterns repeat each other', I am afraid that my interpretation is in conflict with both of them. I cannot see how Thel can be at one and the same time a soul that fears to be embodied and a soul that fears to be disembodied.

C. S. Lewis in contrasting 'allegory' with 'symbolism' uses, as an alternative description of the latter, the word 'sacramentalism'. 'If our passions,' he writes, 'being immaterial, can be copied by material inventions, then it is possible that our material world in its turn is the copy of an invisible world.' This is sheer Platonism, and possibly Blake could be described as an unconscious neo-Platonist, just as Shelley was certainly a conscious one. Some scholars have placed Spenser among the Platonizing poets but a study of *The Faerie Queene* proves at least that this element was not dominant in him. If we turn to our own day, overt Platonizing is rare among writers, though something equivalent can be found in the poems of Rilke and possibly of Edwin Muir. But something more concealed and yet related can be found in unexpected quarters. I have already quoted Esslin's at first sight paradoxical claim that the modern 'playwrights of the Absurd' are essentially religious. I would not concede this about all the playwrights he discusses but I would agree that it is true of Samuel Beckett whose starting-point, paradoxically, is 'nothingness'. Esslin says that one of Beckett's favourite quotations comes from the philosopher Democritus: 'Nothing is more real than nothing.' Now *Godot* and *Endgame* may seem a far cry from Blake but, if we turn to one of the most careful modern analysts of Blake, Mr Northrop Frye, we may find passages in his analysis which could fairly easily be transferred to these works of Beckett's. Take Northrop Frye's account of Ulro, which in the Prophetic Books is the name given to Hell: 'Ulro is the world as it would appear to humanity at the beginning of the Fall, without a single image of human desire, or form of human work, yet established in it—no habitations, no cultivation, nothing but suggestions of indifference, mystery, inscrutable fate, a relentless fight to survive and loneliness.' And some further words of Frye's would apply to another modern work, William Golding's *Pincher Martin*: Ulro, he says, is 'divided between an ego and a vast menacing form of "nature", which to the imagination wavers uncertainly between a paternal and a maternal figure, both equally stupid and cruel'. Some modern critics have even asserted that *Pincher Martin* itself is essentially a study of Hell.

One thing at any rate that Blake has in common with these moderns, in contrast not only with Bunyan but with Spenser, is the very great extension of ambiguity, of meanings that are not only multiple but sometimes even seem contradictory. And it is no good trying to get back to Spenser, though I think a modern poet can learn much from him. Let us glance at some others of our more recent forebears, beginning with Shelley. Shelley is the most obvious example of an undiluted Romantic, the poet as misfit celebrating the hero as misfit—and the poet and the hero are one. *Prometheus Unbound*, which was written thirty years after *The Book of Thel*, is his most ambitious treatment of this theme. In his own Preface to this 'lyrical drama' he admits that he has 'a passion for reforming the world' but is careful at once to add: 'Didactic poetry is my abhorrence; nothing can be equally well expressed in prose that is not tedious and supererogatory in verse.' Now Spenser, in his letter to Raleigh, wrote as if *The Faerie Queene* were meant to be didactic, but whatever his intentions this is not the way it worked out: much of the poem certainly is concerned with moral questions but the morals themselves are not plugged in a pulpit or lecture-room manner. Similarly Spenser for most of the time retains the virtues of prose, which means that he does not deviate too far from the world we live in. Shelley does so deviate, and partly no doubt because he does make an absolute divorce between prose and verse.

One surprising result of this is that, for all Blake's esotericism and consequent ambiguity, I find *The Book of*

Thel more down to earth than *Prometheus Unbound*. One of the few *physical* images in the latter comes in the well-known passage about the poet:

> He will watch from dawn to gloom
> The lake-reflected sun illume
> The yellow bees in the ivy-bloom,
> Nor heed nor see, what things they be;
> But from these create he can
> Forms more real than living man,
> Nurslings of immortality!

So the image is not physical after all; this is 'sacramentalism' with a vengeance. In the same way the landscapes in *Prometheus Unbound* are superficially suggestive of some of those in Goethe's *Faust*, but unlike Goethe's one cannot come to grips with them; the winds in the first Walpurgis-nacht hit you slap in the face, the winds in Shelley remain abstract. As for the *figures* in *Prometheus Unbound*, they make Spenser's Archimago and Duessa and Britomart and Belphoebe and Marinell and even Mutability seem like three-dimensional *characters*. But then, of course, Spenser's Faerie Land is also Elizabethan England, whereas the setting of *Prometheus Unbound* is a highly nebulous cosmos. Shelley's dramatis personae include not only the Earth but the Spirit of the Earth, not only Jupiter but the Phantasm of Jupiter. The poem is full of mysterious sounds and outsize shapes. Typical are the two apparitions in act IV which issue simultaneously from two openings in the forest, the first a winged and white-haired infant in a chariot, the second

> A sphere, which is as many thousand spheres,
> Solid as crystal, yet through all its mass

> Flow, as through empty space, music and light:
> Ten thousand orbs involving and involved,
> Purple and azure, white, and green, and golden,
> Sphere within sphere; and every space between
> Peopled with unimaginable shapes,
> Such as ghosts dream dwell in the lampless deep . . .

This last line in particular but also the whole passage—I have quoted only the beginning of it—are a good example of how Shelley paints the lily. Yet I have to give it my grudging admiration; for here once more we have a poet trying to express the Ineffable. It is a noble effort. (It seems worth mentioning here that most of the best passages in *Prometheus Unbound* are in blank verse. The famous lyrics, much admired by the Victorians, are loose in content and often jingly in their music while the metrical transitions are sometimes very awkward. Once again we find that the form gives away something about the content.)

In *Prometheus Unbound* Shelley, to my mind, was aiming too high; he really does disappear in the 'intense inane'. This is brought home if you compare his *Prometheus* with *Faust*. None of Shelley's other long works is, I think, successful as a whole—he not only is too verbose but also has lapses of taste which are really lapses of common sense. But *Epipsychidion*, for one, has stretches of haunting writing of the vaguer dream kind, while his last and unfinished poem, *The Triumph of Life*, has plenty of good parable writing of the crisper dream kind. In the former, for instance, we meet a false female figure worthy of Spenser:

> One, whose voice was venomed melody
> Sate by a well, under blue nightshade bowers;
> The breath of her false mouth was like faint flowers,
> Her touch was as electric poison . . .

And later there is a very fine nightmare metaphor when

> from coast to coast
> The moving billows of my being fell
> Into a death of ice, immovable . . .

It is worth noting that *Epipsychidion* is written throughout in rhyming couplets which give it some stiffening and also give its fantasy an appearance of continuity—yet another example of the form-content complex.

In *The Triumph of Life* Shelley uses a yet more severe and therefore, if well managed, more sustaining form—terza rima. To match this severer form, the imagery here is on the whole less nebulous and again we meet verse to which we can apply Yeats's epithet 'athletic'. Once more he is often trying to say something that 'has little to do with words at all' but now, thanks to the new strength of the actual writing, the paradox seems more likely to be achieved. Take his very clear description of something by its very nature unclear—the principle of oblivion itself—the 'Shape all light' that carries a glass of Nepenthe:

> And still her feet, no less than the sweet tune
> To which they moved, seemed as they moved to blot
> The thoughts of him who gazed on them; and soon
> All that was, seemed as if it had been not;
> And all the gazer's mind was strewn beneath
> Her feet like embers; and she, thought by thought,
> Trampled its sparks into the dust of death . . .

In a passage like this, which for me represents Shelley at his best, I think we can find that allegory and symbolism are once more intertangled. At any rate it is a highly imaginative example of parable writing.

I took Blake and then moved to Shelley because they are both extreme cases: Blake in that he was a natural visionary (a rare type among poets) and Shelley because he carried further than any of his English contemporaries the Romantic superimposition of the poet's ego on the world. Before passing on to the aftermath of Romanticism I would like to look quickly at Coleridge and Wordsworth. Both of them, in their different ways, were originals and yet with both, when it comes to parable writing, we are back in more normal territory. Wordsworth was an incidental parabolist and his method is sleight-of-hand; he is easy to accept because at first sight his poems appear to be about ordinary things or at least about things which since his time, and largely because of him, have come to be accepted as ordinary. Even when he is recounting experiences of his own which illustrate his far from usual vision of Nature, he delivers them in such an even and matter-of-fact manner that he slips them over on us. He thus provides some remarkable examples of double-level writing. *The Ancient Mariner* and *Christabel* are a very different matter but they also are easier to accept than Blake's Prophetic Books or a great deal of Shelley. In this case the reason seems to be that outwardly at least they fall into a traditional category: they are broadly tales of wonder and in detail they have the suggestiveness which characterizes such tales even when they come from the folk. Percy's *Reliques* had been published in 1765 and from then on, and still more so after Scott, our ballad heritage was to serve as a stimulus and sometimes a quarry to sophisticated poets.

In this corpus of ballad literature, which was now receiving avid attention, there were, alongside the very earthy stories of border raids and vendettas and love affairs, some very striking pieces which brought in the supernatural: these ranged from ghost stories like 'The Wife of Usher's Well' and weird horror stories like 'The Demon Lover' to pieces which have a very strong dream atmosphere like the 'Lykewake Dirge'—pieces which, if not intentionally allegorical, could easily have allegory read into them. Perhaps the best example of this last type is the deservedly famous 'Thomas the Rhymer' with its choice of three roads —to Heaven, to Hell, and to fair Elfland.

> O they rode on and farther on,
>   And they waded through rivers aboon the knee,
> And they saw neither sun nor moon,
>   But they heard the roaring of the sea.
>
> It was mirk mirk night and there was nae stern light
>   And they waded through red blude to the knee;
> For a' the blude that's shed on earth,
>   Rins through the springs o' that countrie.

The Ancient Mariner stands to this rather as *The Faerie Queene* stands to medieval romance. And it is noteworthy that Coleridge here, like Spenser, archaizes and also, again like Spenser, gets away with it. In both cases the archaizing helps to set the poem back the necessary distance from the everyday world. Modern critics, such as Robert Penn Warren and the late Humphry House, the latter in the Clark Lectures for 1951–2, have analysed *The Ancient Mariner* at length, paying particular attention to its imagery. But I would point out that both these critics come up against the allegory–symbol distinction which Coleridge himself had not yet expressed at the date of writing this poem. I agree with House when he writes: 'We may be misled if we start the critique of the "Mariner" and "Kubla Khan" with this disjunction of allegory from symbol in mind. For all allegory involves symbolism, and in proportion as symbolism becomes developed and coherent it tends towards allegory.' This is very much the same point as I have made already, but it is interesting to find House making it about *The Ancient Mariner*. I would only add that once again the 'versification touchstone' works to the poem's credit. Coleridge had lifted some tricks from Percy's *Reliques* but it does not read like pastiche or parody. For a ballad it is exceptionally long but the verse is sufficiently varied to save it from monotony.

The versification touchstone, to my ear, does not work so well for *Christabel*, which I regard as an inferior poem. Coleridge was here making conscious metrical experiments: sometimes they match the story and mood very well, as in the famous repetition

> Is the night chilly and dark?
> The night is chilly, but not dark.

but sometimes it degenerates into a gabble as in the equally famous

> The one red leaf, the last of its clan,
> That dances as often as dance it can,
> Hanging so light, and hanging so high,
> On the topmost twig that looks up at the sky.

The accumulation of short syllables and the switch in the last two lines from dactyls to anapaests may have been meant to suggest the dancing movement of the leaf but the result is rhythmically vulgar. But then I also find in this poem certain vulgarities of content. It was written in the convention of the Gothic tale of terror; Mr Charles Tomlinson indeed maintains that it is the only such tale 'which expresses with any real subtlety the basic pattern of the genre, the struggle between the instinct of death and Eros'. To me, I am afraid, it hovers on the verge of the pseudo-Gothic; but I agree with Mr Tomlinson when he points out what is relevant to my thesis, that none of the protagonists in Coleridge's narrative is in him- or herself complex: all are stock figures and therefore near to allegory; we are back at the negative principle of Too Much Character Spoils the Theme. Mr Tomlinson concludes that 'one is compelled to see the characters as symbols relating to Everyman's condition of inner psychological tension—the evil preying on the good, the sick undermining the healthy'.

Before I pass on to Wordsworth I will mention one other poem of this period, this time, surprisingly, by Byron. It is the poem 'Darkness', which begins with a smack of cards on the table:

I had a dream, which was not all a dream.

This is patently parable writing: we are back in Blake's Ulro and once more anticipating *Endgame*. Unlike, for example, *Manfred*, this poem is felt, and the dour blank verse serves the theme well. The sun has been extinguished and men will do anything to procure temporary light:

Forests were set on fire—but hour by hour
They fell and faded—and the crackling trunks
Extinguish'd with a crash—and all was black.

The poem moves on relentlessly and, without Byron intruding his ego, to its nightmarish and inevitable conclusion:

The world was void,
The populous and the powerful was a lump
Seasonless, herbless, treeless, manless, lifeless.
A lump of death—a chaos of hard clay.
The rivers, lakes, and ocean all stood still,
And nothing stirr'd within their silent depths;
Ships sailorless lay rotting on the sea,
And their masts fell down piecemeal: as they dropp'd
They slept on the abyss without a surge—
The waves were dead; the tides were in their grave,
The Moon, their mistress, had expired before;
The winds were wither'd in the stagnant air,
And the clouds perish'd; Darkness had no need
Of aid from them—She was the Universe.

As Democritus said—and as Samuel Beckett quoted him
—'nothing is more real than nothing'.

And so to Wordsworth. I have mentioned the suggestive comparison made by Dr Janet Spens between a passage in the Twelfth Book of *The Prelude* and a passage in the First Book of *The Faerie Queene*. Dr Spens thinks that this recollection by Wordsworth of an episode in his childhood may have been stimulated by the Spenser passage. But, while admitting that both poets 'are depicting the same mental experience—a gloomy twilight of the mind in which primitive forms move uneasily', she is more concerned to stress the difference in their handling of it, a difference she accounts for by the change of period. She finds that, while both poets show us a girl with a pitcher, for Wordsworth the girl is a mere element in the landscape and it is the landscape that is made to do the work; Spenser on the other hand relies on the girl and her mother, both figures being symbolical. Dr Spens comments that this habit of personification,

looked at with suspicion by Wordsworth, had deteri-
orated in the seventeenth century, was 'dead-alive' throughout the eighteenth, and only came to life again with Blake
and Shelley. Nevertheless Wordsworth is a parabolist of
a kind and we can illustrate the kind by a single poem,
'Resolution and Independence'. Here again we have a
figure in a landscape, the figure of the Leech-gatherer, but
this is far from being merely a simple Wordsworthian
portrait of a simple and long-suffering and deserving old
rustic. Mr W. W. Robson is right in saying that 'the core
of the poem is the "unknown modes of being"', and I
recommend his whole detailed critique of this poem printed
in *Interpretations*. Mr Robson refuses to agree with those
critics, including Coleridge, who complain that the poem is
uneven. On the contrary he finds its prosaicisms justified;
'they perform an essential function, in contrasting the
public world of everyday human experience and human
endurance with the inner world into which Wordsworth has
taken the figure of the Leech-gatherer and made of it a
quantity which cannot be apprehended without uncertainty
and dread.

> While he was talking thus, the lonely place,
> The old Man's shape, and speech—all troubled me.'

I would make two points of my own here. First, that
Wordsworth once again is meeting Spenser, if not on his
own ground, at least halfway in their mutual No Man's
Land:

> And the whole body of the Man did seem
> Like one that I had met with in a dream.

The similarity is underlined when he makes a key point in
an alexandrine:

> Motionless as a cloud the old Man stood,
> That heareth not the loud winds when they call;
> And moveth all together, if it move at all.

Although approached from a quite new direction, this is very like Spenser country—which means an internal country. And the effective use of the alexandrine in this quotation brings me to my second point. In this poem once again, if you use the versification touchstone, you will find that the form is properly matched to the content, that the two are so wedded that they are one body—and one soul. And once again the poem, though essentially a poem, reveals what Mr Eliot demanded, the virtues of good prose. These virtues are more obvious here than in most of the other poems I have quoted in this chapter. Their comparative scarcity among the Romantics may make it less surprising that, as the nineteenth century proceeded, it was the prose writers and the playwrights who produced the best parable writing. I have already suggested that, whether in prose or verse, this sort of writing requires the prose virtues either to compensate for its oddity of content or to evoke a suspension of disbelief or just to make its fantasy take up its bed and walk.

Of the Victorian poets Browning on occasion shows the prose virtues—though on other occasions he shows all the prose vices—but, as far as I remember, he made only one notable excursion into parable, the haunting poem *Childe Roland to the Dark Tower Came*. Here again we find a plain athletic verse serving its purpose admirably. And it is worth comparing the nightmare landscape in this poem with the setting of the Cave of Despair in *The Faerie Queene*. But I will not linger on the freak product of a poet who by

nature was a realist. Instead, to demonstrate the degenera-
tion of parable during the Romantic aftermath, I will take
another Victorian, Christina Georgina Rossetti, whose bent
really was in the direction of allegory. In a short poem she
can sometimes sustain this: *Sleep at Sea*, for instance, which
is built round a single, easily acceptable dream image
and which is supported by a suitably languorous—almost
onomatopoeic—versification. And there is also, less obviously Victorian and more in the Herbert tradition, the
well-known anthology piece beginning

> Does the road wind up-hill all the way?

It is when she tackles a long allegorical poem that Christina
Rossetti reveals how completely she lacks the stamina and
strength for such an undertaking; in fact she lacks the prose
virtues. *Goblin Market* has perhaps a certain charm but is
thin and flags and cloys; it is, however, *The Prince's Progress*,
published in 1866, that is the great example of how not to
write an allegory. This is the story of a prince who sets out
from 'his world-end palace' to find his appointed bride, a
very pre-Raphaelite type. It contains many of the traditional elements, but shockingly emasculated. The versification is sloppy and the imagery imprecise. There is uninten-
tional comedy, as with the beguiling milkmaid, when the
need for a rhyme precipitates a pseudo-significant question:

> Was it milk now, or was it cream?
> Was she a maid, or an evil dream?

And when she attempts a nightmare landscape this, though
not a bad piece of writing, is too generalized compared with
either Browning's or Spenser's. Anyhow she lets it down
by a careless, and again unintentionally comic, bathos:

Untrodden before, untrodden since:
Tedious land for a social Prince . . .

After crossing the nightmare land and wasting some time with an alchemist, the prince, who had previously wasted time with the milkmaid, begins once more to hanker for female company. 'It's oh for a second maiden, at least,' he cries. And sure enough he finds one but she is a poor substitute for Calypso or for the seductresses in the folk tales. The upshot and the moral of it all is that he arrives too late at his destination. In this poem the great ancient theme of the Quest has come to a sorry pass: it has been sentimentalized. And by this I do not mean that Christina Rossetti was insincere; she certainly was nothing of the sort. Insincerity is one of the commonest causes of sentimentality but lack of head can cause it as well as lack of heart. And when I say 'lack of head' I again do not mean that this poet had a low I.Q. Lack of head here implies a lack in her personal experience and knowledge and a background lack in the society and period in which she lived.

To develop this point about sentimentality we can take a writer of prose whom some people, mistakenly I think, would like to dismiss as a sentimentalist (but he is very hard to dismiss). I mean Hans Andersen, who was publishing his first fairy tales thirty years before Christina Rossetti published *The Prince's Progress*. Though he does not—at least directly—belong to English literature, I introduce him here because he serves as a bridge to the so-called children's books with which I shall be largely concerned in my next chapter. The Grimm collection of folk tales had been published some twenty years earlier, but in feeling Hans Andersen is nearer to Christina Rossetti than to Grimm.

The heroes in Grimm just want to get their girl—or a fortune or whatever it is—but the quests of Andersen's heroes and heroines have often the same spiritual quality as that of the Rossetti prince. The Andersen quests, however, are much more interesting and vivid and not, I maintain, sentimental. This is because, as in Bunyan's *Pilgrim's Progress*, though the fantastic story may be primary, the characters in the story are filled out from the author's own experience and observation. And, again as in Bunyan, there is a saving humour—which can also rank as a prose virtue. Moreover, those who know Danish attach enormous importance to Andersen's prose style which, it seems, is at once subtle and simple and equally suited to lyrical evocations and to comedy.

Andersen as a person was neurotic and lonely; during the rest of the century there were to be many writers in many countries who were both. Another writer for children, Edward Lear, was like Andersen in at least one respect, in that, in spite of his loneliness, he was always too frightened to ask anyone to marry him. The resulting self-pity comes out in many of Lear's nonsense poems but it is transmuted in them—even in 'The Yonghy-Bonghy-Bo'—and so ceases in fact to be self-pity. Andersen's melancholy comes out in some of the sadder stories, notably *The Little Mermaid*, but this again is transmuted. What in Andersen is particularly relevant to my thesis is that many of his stories are more patently allegorical than almost any writing of the time, whether in poetry or in drama—the novels for the time being had pretty well sold out to realism. Such stories include *The Little Mermaid* itself, *The Snow Queen* (a very good example of the quest), *The Nightingale*, *The Shadow* and, on a more domestic plane, *The Ugly Duckling*. But this allegory never creaks; children indeed do not, consciously at least, notice it. This is because, as Auden and Pearson put it, 'the images used do in fact have a symbolic value over and above their allegorical use'. In *The Ugly Duckling* or *The Shadow* or *The Nightingale* Andersen may have been thinking of himself but the story has taken over. As Yeats wrote in a late poem,

> Players and painted stage took all my love
> And not those things that they were emblems of.

From Yeats this was perhaps a surprising admission, since he was always fussing with abstractions and inventing emblems for them. But it would not have been surprising if Andersen had said it. He was obviously not a man for abstractions; he was above all a showman who could make even puppets come to life. I have suggested that by his time there were good reasons why parable writing should be practised by prose writers rather than poets; similar reasons possibly apply today. But there were also historical reasons in the nineteenth century why certain very adult things could best be said in books which, nominally at least, were meant for children. In this country that century saw an efflorescence of such books. It is a peculiar phenomenon which I shall discuss next.

IV

THE VICTORIANS

I HAVE now to discuss some of the nineteenth-century heirs of Romanticism. Bulking large among these will be the writers of so-called children's books. They are more relevant to my purpose—and more truly in the Romantic tradition—than either the Victorian poets like Tennyson, Browning, Arnold and their successors or most of the Victorian novelists. Dickens, I think, may be a partial exception but I shall not go into his peculiar case. I would only suggest here that in his so-called 'poetic' passages, which admittedly contain most of his worst writing, Dickens is encroaching on the kind of mystery which calls for parable rather than realism (look at the death of Little Dombey). It was Dickens's awareness of this that made him write so badly. He did it, I suggest, for the right reasons.

As regards parable writing in general, we seem already to have come to certain tentative conclusions. (1) The parabolist more often than not is concerned with the creation of a special world: as in *The Faerie Queene* such a world can be very true to life, but to the inner life of man rather than to his life in an objective context. Of course there are many exceptions to this: the cruder kind of allegory, what Northrop Frye calls 'naïve' allegory, can be used to cover subjects from which the inner life is excluded—such things as General Elections. After all, political cartoons are often downright allegorical in their method.

(2) This preoccupation with an inner reality naturally means that parable writing has often a strong spiritual, or indeed a mystical, element. Mr Esslin, as we saw, found this a characteristic of the contemporary 'Theatre of the Absurd'.

(3) Esslin also pointed out that many of his playwrights, Beckett in particular, are much concerned with the problem of identity. We have noticed that in *The Faerie Queene*, for instance, two characters can be merged in one or one can be dispersed or expanded into several: this is what happens in dreams. A writer I discuss below, George MacDonald, uses this dream method regularly. In other forms of parable writing, as in *Everyman* and in Beckett's prose works such as *Malone Dies*, identity is tackled by a process of elimination; it is what Peer Gynt does to himself in the onion-peeling scene: 'When am I going to get to the heart?'

(4) In contrast to the realistic novel or play which lays such stress upon character, parable writing, as we have seen, is more concerned with theme, this theme very often, as in *Pilgrim's Progress*, finding its embodiment through a very strong story-line. Thus theme and story often coalesce: if you discard the story of *Pilgrim's Progress*, you are left with the disembodied theme, i.e. with the matter of a bleak and quite unoriginal sermon. The hero in parable writing tends to be Everyman. I suggested that this was true of Spenser's Red Cross Knight, even though he is supposed to be the personification of Holiness; it is obviously true of Peer Gynt and to some extent of the main characters in the first three novels of William Golding.

(5) In so far as parable writing is akin to dreams, it tempts one, just as religious myths and folk tales do, to look

below its 'manifest' content for a 'latent' content which can then be interpreted in terms of one's favourite modern psychologist. This is an amusing proceeding but can be very destructive. Just as in a poem the manifest content, which is inseparable from the *form* of the poem, cannot be reduced to something in the Unconscious which occasioned it, no more, of course, in the works I am considering can the image, whether it is object or event, be reduced without residue to that of which it is an image. Whether the parabolist was unconscious of some psychological origin of his images or, as with Spenser's historical allegory, only too conscious of a theme to be given a new body, it is this new body that counts. The writer's mythopoeic faculty transcends both his personal background and his so-called message: Duessa can never be reduced into Mary, Queen of Scots, nor Alice, swimming in the pool of her own tears, to a nostalgic, if unconscious, yearning for the forbidden joys of bed-wetting.

(6) It follows from the five points already made that the parabolist, whether he uses prose or verse, is following a poetic rather than a documentary procedure. In so far as his creations are fantasy, this fantasy can belong to either of Coleridge's two categories of works of 'Imagination' and 'Fancy'. The greatest traditional myths, such as those of Orpheus and Eurydice or the Rape of Persephone, are in this sense works of Imagination: the myth, that is, appears inevitable and fulfils a need in the reader that he may or may not have been aware of. The fantasies of mere Fancy, on the other hand, seem not inevitable but arbitrary; they have surface but no depth; they amuse but they do not nourish; they are almost a form of doodling. These two kinds are often found in the same work.

(7) Since the parabolist is much nearer to the poet than to the more objective types of prose writer such as the documentary novelist, one would expect the formal elements to be of correspondingly greater importance in his work. Here, however, it is difficult to generalize. We have noticed already that sometimes, even in *The Faerie Queene*, a plain, almost matter-of-fact style is paradoxically appropriate to a far from ordinary content. But a parabolist cannot be confined to one particular kind of style. When faults on the formal side are obvious, it is very likely, though not certain, that this indicates faults in the writer's total conception.

(8) This business of a writer's 'total conception' brings us back to the difficult question of belief, which I linked with experience and attitude. It is significant that the three children's writers whom I am about to consider were all practising Christians (indeed they were all clergymen, though in a difficult period for that profession). It seems possible that, in order to achieve parable writing of the order of Imagination rather than of mere Fancy, the parabolist must have some sort of world-view which engages his deepest feelings. A modern case in point is William Golding whom I shall discuss later.

I mentioned in the last chapter a most untypical poem by Browning, *Childe Roland to the Dark Tower Came*. Browning was primarily a documentary poet, but this unwonted excursion into fantasy emerges as far more serious than most Victorian fantasies in verse. Compare it, for instance, with a poem written a few years earlier by Matthew Arnold, *The Forsaken Merman*. The merman, you will remember, with his children had been abandoned by his human wife, who had returned to a life on land in order not to lose her soul. It is a very similar theme to that of one of the great modern fairy stories, *The Little Mermaid* by Hans Andersen. But whereas in Andersen the crux of the story is the great gulf separating the people of the sea from human beings, a separation which is rich in symbolic overtones, Arnold's forsaken merman might be any old forsaken husband: apart from his tail there is nothing basically different about him. The opportunities are missed and the poem lacks depth. Once again we find that this inadequacy in the total conception is reflected on the formal side: the poem is badly organized and the continually changing rhythms are on the whole inappropriate and therefore frivolous. When we turn to Browning's *Childe Roland* we find there, too, certain technical flaws: Browning here, as so often, seems to like writing awkwardly just for the sake of it. But the total conception is there and the poem, as a whole, embodies it adequately. It has the depth—the universality, if you like—which *The Forsaken Merman* lacks.

This is partly because Browning, as is obvious from his documentary poems such as 'My Last Duchess', had much more *dramatic* sense than Arnold. He begins, in a way which would have delighted the ancients, by plunging *in medias res:*

My first thought was, he lied in every word.

We find that we are in the middle of a Quest, a traditional one complete with knight errant, and yet it is a quest with a difference. The basic paradox, almost anticipating the playwrights of the Absurd, is established near the beginning:

I hardly tried now to rebuke the spring
My heart made, finding failure in its scope.

Then, as in dreams, we have the sudden transformation of landscape:

> So, quiet as despair, I turned from him,
>   That hateful cripple, out of his highway
>   Into the path he pointed. All the day
> Had been a dreary one at best, and dim
> Was settling to its close, yet shot one grim
>   Red leer to see the plain catch its estray.

> For mark! no sooner was I fairly found
>   Pledged to the plain, after a pace or two,
>   Than, pausing to throw backward a last view
> To the safe road, 'twas gone; grey plain all round:
> Nothing but plain to the horizon's bound.
>   I might go on; nought else remained to do.

Browning proceeds to sketch a nightmare landscape, a waste land, in which, however, the surprises continue—as indeed they do in nightmares:

> A sudden little river crossed my path
> As unexpected as a serpent comes.

It would be hard to find allegorical significance in this river but it is certainly pregnant as symbol—'so petty yet so spiteful!' Later, after some forced or superfluous similes, there comes the greatest transformation of all:

> For, looking up, aware I somehow grew
>   'Spite of the dusk, the plain had given place
>   All round to mountains—with such name to grace
> Mere ugly heights and heaps now stolen in view.

And then the scales drop from the hero's eyes:

> Burningly it came on me all at once,
> This was the place!

He has reached the Dark Tower, his destination where even defeat is an achievement. One could almost argue that in this one poem Browning is anticipating the Existentialists; but it is more to my purpose here to point out that this is one of the few really successful pieces of parable writing in Victorian *verse*. (I am about to come on to its parallels in prose.) Once again, though the details such as 'the sudden little river' cannot—or at least should not—be allegorically pinpointed, the poem as a whole stands up because it has a spine of allegory. And once again, whatever its technical flaws, its general tone and texture are functional, whereas in Tennyson's Arthurian poems, for instance, although the rhythms and the general sound of the verse are much more agreeable, they are not appropriate to their subject.

Childe Roland was published in 1855. Soon after this came a great efflorescence of English fantasies in prose, some of it, though not all of it, intended—at least nominally—for children. Hans Andersen had pioneered this line of country some twenty years before and was not to die until 1875. Before then England had produced several writers who in one respect or another were rivals to Andersen, though very different from him—and from each other. In less than ten years, from 1863 to 1872, the following English books were published for the first time: *The Water Babies*, the two Alice books, Lear's *Nonsense Songs and Stories*, and *The Princess and the Goblin* by George MacDonald. Lear I am going to omit. As has often been pointed out, by Aldous Huxley among others, he should be treated seriously as a Victorian poet, stylistically comparable to his friend Tennyson. Lear's 'nonsense' is the disguise of a man who was congenitally shy: the Dong and the Yonghy-Bonghy-Bo, for example, obviously stand for Lear himself. A poem like 'The Jumblies' is escapist (I am not using the word pejoratively) and so naturally appeals to the escapist in all of us. But what I am more concerned with here is other aspects of Everyman. So I shall now take a look—in that order—at Kingsley, Lewis Carroll and MacDonald. All three have a strong element that *could* be called escapist but, as is not the case in Lear, this is complicated with other very different elements, satirical, moral, or mystical.

First of all, a book that is now unduly neglected, *The Water Babies*, which was published just over a hundred years ago. It is Kingsley's own fault that it is neglected, since it is one of the most uneven and ragbaggy books in the language. This is not just because the first chapter was written in half an hour, allegedly for his five-year-old son, nor because the idiom of Rabelais, whom he read through every year, had gone to his head. It is much more because, as he himself admitted in a letter, he had tried to cram into it all the questions of the day 'wrapped up in seeming Tom-Fooleries'. The Alice books also contain their echoes of contemporary academic disputes but these are not allowed to interfere with the story. Lewis Carroll always fuses the parts into the whole; he jumps about but unlike Kingsley he does not, in the proper sense, digress; above all he does not stand outside his story to moralize—which means, paradoxically, that he does not come crashing into it to moralize. In *The Water Babies* Kingsley does this all the time, and in a story which, potentially, had many of the virtues of a myth it is a very serious fault. As Mr John Wain has written of William Golding's novels, 'no myth contains comment on its own action'.

If we discount the digressions—and they are a great deal to discount—*The Water Babies* appears compounded about fifty-fifty of a Victorian morality and a wishful fantasy. The second aspect is what appeals to children—and to most adults. Even if we ignore the Freudian derivation of dreams of swimming (such dreams, according to Freud, often indicate a wish to return to the womb), the sea remains for us—though maybe this only dates from the Romantic Revival—an enormous symbol of escape and freedom. And for Kingsley, an addict of natural history who had been much struck by Darwin's brand-new theory of evolution, the sea meant not only escape but escape back to the mother. Life had begun in the waters—this point had been made, long before Darwin, in the second part of Goethe's *Faust*—and therefore to return to the waters was almost a return to prelapsarian purity. Even Ibsen, in an early note for *The Wild Duck*, wrote: 'Human beings are sea-creatures —like the wild duck—not land creatures.' Mr W. H. Auden in his book *The Enchafèd Flood* (1951), a book of typically staccato criticism subtitled 'The Romantic Iconography of the Sea', stresses the new attitude to the sea introduced by the Romantics. The Romantic attitude to the sea is, though he does not use the word, *dialectical*: the sea, Auden says, is 'the Alpha of existence, the symbol of potentiality', but it also remains what the ancients thought it, the first and last symbol of primeval chaos, of the indefatigable destroyer. It corresponds to the figure of Siva in Hindu mythology. In *The Water Babies* Kingsley, unlike Melville in *Moby Dick*, to whom Auden pays deserved attention, concentrated on the first aspect. For Tom, the brutalized little chimney sweep who becomes a water baby, the sea is first and foremost an escape from the horrors of human life on land. But in the latter part of the book the sea becomes also the setting for a Quest. We are told that it is a difficult quest but Tom seems to take it in his stride— or in his breast-stroke. However, since this quest is imposed upon him by the mysterious female figure who is half fairy godmother and half recording angel, we should pay as much attention to the morality part of the story as we do to the wishful or nostalgic fantasy. Kingsley had a passion for natural history for its own sake: hence, in this book, his vivid descriptions of caddises and dragonflies, seals and lobsters. But he was also a kind of pantheist-cum-moralist, the Anglican Church's answer, one might say, to Wordsworth. It was in this capacity that he invented the formidable fairy Mrs Bedonebyasyoudid who, as the story progresses, becomes more and more equated with her beautiful sister Mrs Doasyouwouldbedoneby. She is one of those immortal dedicated creatures of whom we can meet many in the fantasies of George MacDonald.

It is of course the moral element in *The Water Babies* that puts it in a different class from many other children's books such as, say, *The Wind in the Willows*—or, for that matter, *Peter Pan*, that coy and frivolous story, which is largely frivolous because it is coy. Although the second part of *The Water Babies*, the Quest part, is aesthetically inferior to the first, the 'escapist' part, it is doubtful if Kingsley, being the sort of man he was, would have written the book at all if Tom had not been foredoomed to work out his own salvation through a moral struggle with himself. There are eight chapters in *The Water Babies*. It is not till chapter 3 that we get into the water and it is not till chapter 5 that

Tom's eyes are opened and he can see the other water babies who have been around him all the time. The reason for this eye-opening promotion is that he has done a good turn to a lobster trapped in a lobster pot (*mutatis mutandis*, we can compare in *The Ancient Mariner* the effect of the Mariner's blessing of the water snakes). Immediately after meeting his 'peer-group' of water babies, he meets the two fairy sisters who share the supervision of them. Tom has now entered the kindergarten of the sea, his first experience of community life, and from now on, since Kingsley is a moralist, the beginning of the Quest is just a matter of time.

Sure enough, at the start of chapter 6 Tom starts stealing sweets and is suitably punished by coming out all over prickles. 'For you must know', says Mrs Bedoneby-asyoudid, 'that people's souls make their bodies.' Tom repents quite quickly but he is not let off so easily. He is told that he needs a schoolmistress who will teach him how to get rid of his prickles. By a sentimental twist, this 'schoolmistress' turns out to be Ellie, the pretty little girl whom in chapter 1 Tom had seen in the big house where he was sweeping the chimneys. Since then Ellie, like Tom, has in the ordinary sense of the word died, but instead of becoming a water baby she appears to have gone straight to heaven from which she has now been seconded to cure Tom of his prickles. Ellie is a case of *das Ewig-Weibliche*, the creative or redemptive Female Principle—again there are many parallels in George MacDonald—but I find her unsatisfactory. The manner of her death in chapter 4 was a highly contrived coincidence and her relationship with Tom at the end of the book is obscure. However, she does pull her weight in the plot both by curing Tom of his prickles

86

and after that by inspiring him to undertake his quest in search of his wicked old sweep-master, Grimes, who also by now is dead and confined in an original kind of purgatory, the punishment fitting the crime. Before Tom sets off, Mrs Bedonebyasyoudid also encourages him with a really old-fashioned piece of moral allegory: 'the history of the great and famous nation of the Doasyoulikes, who came away from the country of Hardwork, because they wanted to play on the Jew's harp all day long'. The ruthless humour of this is Bunyanesque, and Kingsley also reminds us of Bunyan when he loads the dice and sets these self-indulgent people to live on a burning mountain. Their history is an example of evolution in reverse: the Doasyoulikes degenerate into gorillas and the last one is shot by M. du Chailler. With this moral chapter 6 ends and Tom is ready to set out on his Quest.

The first stages of the Quest, in chapter 7, are full of concrete invention and still have a rich tang of the sea. One of the best characters here is the last of the Gairfowl: 'a very grand old lady, she was, full three feet high, and bolt upright, like some old Highland chieftainess'. Both in his portrayal of this creature and in her conversation, which is both garrulous and snobbish, Kingsley reminds one of Hans Andersen: 'In the days of my ancestors no birds ever thought of having wings, and did very well without; and now they all laugh at me because I keep to the good old fashion.' I have already remarked that in *Pilgrim's Progress* the naturalism of the dialogue saves the characters from being mere vehicles of abstract ideas. In my next author, Lewis Carroll, the dialogue is of primary importance, and we shall find when we come to modern playwrights such as

Beckett and Pinter that once again it is their dialogue which helps us to the necessary suspension of disbelief. If Kingsley had only been content with his ear for human conversation and his eye for natural history, he would not have lapsed as badly as he does in the last chapter of this book where the moralizing rhetorician takes over. But before that, while we are still in chapter 7, between Kingsley the natural historian and Kingsley the moralist we have a short but very important innings by Kingsley the pantheist. This is when Tom has passed 'the white gate that never was opened yet' and comes to the pool of Mother Carey where 'she sits making old beasts into new all the year round'. Mother Carey's pool is Kingsley's Garden of Adonis and she herself is represented as an enthroned white marble lady sitting quite still with her chin upon her hand. '"I am never more busy than I am now," she said, without stirring a finger.' Here the invention is still concrete and therefore acceptable.

In the eighth and last chapter, unfortunately, when Tom reaches 'The Other-end-of-Nowhere', Kingsley switches to a quite different kind of writing, the kind at which Dean Swift was very good but Kingsley is not. Thus we visit Waste-paper-land and the Island of Polypragmosyne: 'There Tom saw ploughs drawing horses, nails driving hammers, birds' nests taking boys, books making authors, bulls keeping china-shops . . ..' As rhetoric some of this may be effective but all these abstractions are out of key with the main story. It takes far too long to get to Grimes and the end of the Quest. After which, to get Tom 'back again', we have the typical metaphorical miracle of the backstairs, contrived by Mrs Bedonebyasyoudid. 'So she tied the

bandage on his eyes with one hand, and with the other she
took it off. "Now", she said, "you are safe up the stairs."'
(This again is very similar to the many dreamlike trans-
formations or transportations which happen equally quickly
in George MacDonald.) The ascent of the backstairs almost
concludes *The Water Babies*. All that remains is the confusing reunion of Tom and Ellie, both now fully grown up,
and a last flash of the more mystical Kingsley evoked by the
old headmistress of a fairy. Mrs Bedonebyasyoudid turns
out to be also Mrs Doasyouwouldbedoneby and also Mother
Carey and also a wandering Irishwoman who had befriended
Tom when he was still a little chimney sweep:

And when they looked she was neither of them, and yet all of
them at once.
'My name is written in my eyes, if you have eyes to see it
there.'
... but the children could not read her name; for they were
dazzled, and hid their faces in their hands.

This transfiguration or near-apotheosis of the ugly old fairy
again has its parallels, which I will come to shortly, in
George MacDonald. It also reminds me of the last section
of Hans Andersen's story, *The Snow Queen*, where the little
lost boy Kay is found 'at his intellectual ice puzzle' by
Gerda who has long been (again the theme of the Quest) in
search of him. Their reunion affects even the jigsaw-like
pieces of ice, which 'danced for joy all round them, and
when they grew tired and lay down again, they formed the
very letters the Snow Queen had told him he must find out
if he were to be his own master and she were to give him
the whole world and a new pair of skates'. Note here yet
again that lightness of touch which precludes sentimentality.

For the word which is formed by the pieces of ice is the word 'Eternity'.

I have several times compared Kingsley with George MacDonald. Before I come to this extraordinary writer, whose mythopoeic faculty is far greater than Kingsley's, I want to say just a little about Lewis Carroll whose artistry is far greater than Kingsley's. Compared with *The Water Babies*, the Alice books—not surprisingly perhaps—are pretty *dry* books. And at first glance one might think they should not be included at all in the same group as either *The Water Babies* or the fantasies of MacDonald. It is only too easy to think of them as works of mere light entertainment, turned out almost as an exercise by a child-loving don who happened to be also a logician, a parodist and a punster. But Alice was not a mere exercise: Carroll himself wrote afterwards that 'every idea and nearly every word of the dialogue came of itself'. There is a good deal more to the Alice books than wit and playful patterns: in *Wonderland* for example Alice's recurrent changes of size are a functional device, what would now be called a gimmick, of the same kind as Swift's devices in *Gulliver's Travels*. But, gimmick or not, this is also the sort of thing that happens in dreams, and Carroll's explicit presentation of both the Alice stories as dreams is also, whether gimmick or not, a giveaway. Once more we are up against the Irreducible Surface. Take even the parodies: the White Knight's song cannot be reduced to a parody of Wordsworth's 'Resolution and Independence'. And the Red Queen, who was based on Alice Liddell's governess, Miss Prickett, cannot be reduced to Miss Prickett. As for the heroine herself, she is much more of a character than is usual in a fairy story—no doubt because she was copied from Alice Liddell—but at the same time she is Everyman or rather Everychild. The books are full of ideas, the ideas that would come naturally to a mathematical don, but, unlike so many of Kingsley's ideas, by the time they have got in on the act, they really *are* in the act, they are concrete. This is so even with the word-play: 'I only wish *I* had such eyes,' the King remarked in a fretful tone. 'To be able to see Nobody! And at that distance too! Why, it's as much as I can do to see real people by this light!' I have already remarked on the importance of Carroll's dialogue, which includes Alice's conversations with herself: it is one of the main constituents of the special world of these books. Technically, Carroll is much less dated than either Kingsley or MacDonald and, unlike them, can be regarded as a forerunner of certain only too adult writers of the twentieth century—Kafka, for instance, or Pinter. In these you find the same sort of blend of ratiocination and absurdity.

This special world of Carroll's, I must repeat, is a dream world which hits the reader very palpably. People with a smattering of Freud might laugh at Alice's long fall at the beginning of the first book and even more when she *floats* down *stairs* in the second book. But whether Lewis Carroll (or perhaps here I should say the Reverend Charles Dodgson) was sexually rather peculiar or not, the plant and the flower once more cannot be reduced to the seed and the dung. One of the settings in *Alice in Wonderland* that is particularly true to dream is the very first place Alice enters after she has fallen down the very deep well, that 'long, low hall, which was lit up by a row of lamps hanging from the roof'. There are two important points about this hall:

there are doors all round it (of normal size) which are locked; behind a curtain there is a very much smaller door which is also locked. Alice finds the key to this door and it reveals to her 'the loveliest garden you ever saw', but she is too big to get through it. (Freud can of course be dragged in again here if you think it worth it.) She does not enter this garden till a long way on in the story and then, to my mind, it is rather a let-down. But, so long as she was in the hall wishing to get out, the situation was most meaningful. It may seem absurd, but Keats's famous letter about the Chamber of Maiden-thought has always reminded me of this passage in Alice.

One other *motif* which keeps recurring in the Alice books is a frequent characteristic of parable writing, for instance *Peer Gynt*: I mean Alice's concern about her own identity or the aspersions cast on her identity by the creatures she meets. In the Wonderland book, for example, whenever Alice is asked to recite a piece of verse that she knows very well, she finds to her alarm, as she says, that the words 'all come different': this makes her feel that she must be different too. She is, of course, and yet she still remains herself, Alice. This is a paradox which she cannot under-stand but it is perfectly clear to the Cheshire Cat. '"We're all mad here," the Cat says. "I'm mad. You're mad." "How do you know I'm mad?" said Alice. "You must be", said the Cat, "or you wouldn't come here." Alice didn't think that proved it at all.' Alice didn't think that proved it at all but it is in fact proof conclusive—as anyone must know who has ever been in love. The Cheshire Cat is probably the most mature character in *Alice in Wonderland*: this is why he has the last laugh—or rather the last grin—at the expense of the Queen and her Executioner.

In *Through the Looking-Glass*, which came six years later, identity is still a sore point with Alice. Thanks to the framework of the game of chess, this book is more of a deliberate quest than its predecessor. Alice who begins as a pawn has got to become a queen. Her second move takes her into 'the wood where things have no names'. Here she makes friends with a Fawn who asks her

'What do you call yourself?'
'I wish I knew!' thought poor Alice. She answered, rather sadly, 'Nothing just now.'
'Think again,' it said: 'that won't do.'
Alice thought, but nothing came of it. 'Please would you tell me what *you* call yourself?' she said timidly. 'I think that might help a little.'
'I'll tell you, if you'll come a little further on,' the Fawn said. 'I can't remember here.'

They go a little further on and emerge from the wood.

'I'm a Fawn!' it cried out in a voice of delight. 'And, dear me! you're a human child!'
A sudden look of alarm came into its beautiful brown eyes, and in another moment it had darted away at full speed.

This passage is not just the *jeu d'esprit* of an Oxford don who has studied the traditional conundrums of philosophy: it is also the rather moving dramatization of one's everyday discovery that selfhood cuts one off from the rest of the universe. In the next chapter Alice's identity is challenged again but from a different angle. They are looking at the Red King who is sound asleep, snoring, in a wood.

'He's dreaming now,' said Tweedledee: 'and what do you think he's dreaming about? . . . Why about you! . . . And if he left off dreaming about you, where do you suppose you'd be?'

'Where I am now, of course,' said Alice.

'Not you!' Tweedledee retorted contemptuously. 'You'd be nowhere. Why, you're only a sort of a thing in his dream!'

Three chapters later we meet another variation where the unicorn, who always thought human children were fabulous monsters, proposes a bargain to Alice: 'If you believe in me, I'll believe in you.' Thanks to Lewis Carroll's ease of manner the reader may not notice that this is all near the bone: after all, even the most hardheaded business man has a solipsist inside him somewhere. And the final moral perhaps comes from Tweedledee and is at the expense of the whole Romantic Movement (it is the sort of remark Mephistopheles sometimes makes to Faust): 'You won't make yourself a bit realler by crying.'

These passages, and many others from the Alice books, bear out, I think, Humphry House's remark (see p. 67) that 'in proportion as symbolism becomes developed and coherent it tends towards allegory'. Here again, however, it would be a mistake—it is a mistake very often even with Spenser—to try to pin down the allegory in any detail. And this would be even more of a mistake with George Mac-Donald whose son wrote of his father's 'symbolic utterance' —'To him a symbol was far more than an arbitrary outward and visible sign of an abstract conception: its high virtue lay in a common *substance* with the idea presented.' This is what, in contrast to allegory, C. S. Lewis called 'sacramentalism', but Lewis himself, who was a great admirer of MacDonald, describes his brand of fantasy as something 'that hovers between the allegorical and the mythopoeic'. Another great admirer, G. K. Chesterton, also labours rather unhelpfully the distinction between MacDonald's 'sort of mystery' and 'mere allegory' or 'commonplace allegory'. Most of the works I have been discussing are neither 'mere' nor 'commonplace', but they are still—as Humphry House would have maintained—to some extent allegorical even though this allegory, as in *The Ancient Mariner*, can hardly be disentangled from the other elements in the work. MacDonald was a great admirer of the German Romantic poet Novalis, of whom I know nothing, but among the English Romantics the one most obviously akin to him is Shelley.

MacDonald's writings are not to everyone's taste—I myself find much of *Phantastes* unpalatable—partly because he is not essentially a writer. Both Chesterton and Lewis admit that he often writes badly—most of his verse is deplorable—and Lewis explains that the sort of myth which MacDonald creates so lavishly 'does not essentially exist in *words* at all'; this is similar to what Miss Raine maintains of Blake, that his dream figures are drawn from a layer that lies below words. If this premise is accepted, it follows, as Lewis points out, that MacDonald's myths might come over just as well in some other medium such as the film. However, as he happened to write them, let us consider them as literature, for in the realm of parable writing no one went further than MacDonald in the whole of the nineteenth century. MacDonald is thought of today as a children's writer; but his first and last books of fantasy, *Phantastes* (1858) and *Lilith* (1895), far from being intended for children, are the parable equivalents of the intimate journals of someone who is basically a mystic but also constitutionally melancholy. It is significant that both of these books are written in the first person. Technically, MacDonald's main problem was that of the mystical poets, how to express the Ineffable, and like many mystical poets he tries to do this by piling up sensuous detail (notice particularly the use he makes of precious stones). But even in MacDonald, especially in the children's books, we find, as in Bunyan and Andersen, the dry aside, the flat prosy statement or the touch of humour which serve as correctives to what might seem overlush or overjewelled. Thus the Bunyanesque note is struck in *The Princess and Curdie* when he is describing a corrupt society: 'There were even certain quacks in the city who advertised pills for enabling people to think well of themselves, and some few bought of them, but most laughed, and said, with evident truth, that they did not require them.' And in *The Golden Key*, where the hero and heroine, Mossy and Tangle, are enabled to communicate with the beasts, birds and insects, we hear the Andersen note: the squirrels, for instance, turn out to be kind, 'but the bees were selfish and rude, justifying themselves on the ground that Tangle and Mossy were not subjects of their queen, and charity must begin at home, though indeed they had not one drone in their poorhouse at the time'. But these are minor matters: what is unique in MacDonald is his passionately spiritual attitude to the universe and his prolific invention of symbols to embody it. It should be noted that with him, as with Kingsley but much more so, the stories involve very serious moral issues, which are contingent not on Law but on Grace.

MacDonald was a great admirer of *Pilgrim's Progress*, but Bunyan's story is traditional homespun in comparison with his own fantastically novel and highly complicated embroideries. This complexity reaches an extreme in his last fantasy *Lilith*. I can here do no more than mention some of his basic themes and symbols, and I doubt if this will convince anyone that Chesterton was not mad when he wrote that of all the stories he had read *The Princess and the Goblin* was 'the most like life'. It will be remembered that C. S. Lewis said something similar about *The Faerie Queene*. The life that these two critics discover in these two works is human life as seen, or felt, or divined from the inside. All MacDonald's fantasies are spiritual explorations, and he could not have written them, any more than Bunyan could have written *Pilgrim's Progress*, if he had not held certain beliefs. The orthodox Christian belief in personal immortality is complicated in him by an individual and mystical vision of a universe which can only be understood by the assumption of extra dimensions, a universe where, regardless of time and space, two or more worlds are continually superimposed. This special vision MacDonald, like the mystical poets, could only attempt to convey through physical imagery, but with him, as his son pointed out, it is essential to remember that such images are never mere algebraic symbols. 'The rose,' he explained in a conversation reported by his son, 'when it gives some glimmer of the freedom for which a man hungers, does so because of its *substantial* unity with the man, each in degree being a signature of God's immanence.' MacDonald's son says that, when his father wrote *Lilith*, 'he was possessed by a feeling . . . that it was a mandate direct from God'.

This being so, it is worth noting that MacDonald does not talk about God, let alone Christ, in his parable writing. Goethe, on the other hand, who was not a Christian, could round off part two of *Faust* only by unleashing a whole

97

traditional Catholic phantasmagoria. As Faust ascends to heaven one of the first people he passes is a 'Pater Ecstaticus' floating up and down in the air: he is rapidly succeeded by Pater Profundus, Pater Seraphicus, a Chorus of Blessed Boys:

> Innocents—who, born at midnight
> With half-opened soul and brain,
> Were at once your parents' loss,
> Were at once the angels' gain—

then by a whole assortment of angels, a Doctor Marianus, a Chorus of Penitent Women, including the long-lost Gretchen, and finally the Mater Gloriosa. I find this unsatisfactory and, indeed, embarrassing, and think MacDonald took the better course. But MacDonald's course requires a very unusual gift of sheer invention, which fortunately he possessed. A few of his minor creations appear arbitrary and therefore fail to pull their weight— some of his monsters, for instance, might have been knocked up by Hieronymus Bosch on an off day—but on the whole the stream of invention flows astonishingly fresh without any sign of failing: compare the last scene of *Faust* either with the last scene of *The Golden Key* or with the Ascent to the City near the end of *Lilith*. As for Goethe's speciality, *das Ewig-Weibliche*, I think MacDonald's extraordinary supernatural females compare very well with either Gretchen or Goethe's Virgin Mary. It would be more appropriate to compare the mysterious powers known as 'The Mothers', except that Goethe has not really told us enough about them. They are the conferrers of magical gifts, and so are these strange creations of MacDonald's such as the Old Lady in *The Princess and the Goblin* who

98

can be seen only by those who have faith and who then sometimes appears as a beautiful young lady. Other examples are the beautiful old women in *Phantastes* and *The Golden Key*, and Mara, the daughter of Adam and Eve, in *Lilith*.

These creatures, who are neither goddesses nor angels nor enchantresses nor fairies but something of all four, exist in a way outside normal time but slip into our time or allow us to slip into theirs, in order to do their good works— and they are all indefatigable workers. The other world to which they belong seems to be ruled by the two great principles of Love and Death—what C. S. Lewis rightly calls 'a good death'. These worlds are entered from ours by something in the nature of a conjuring trick. In both *The Princess and the Goblin* and *Lilith* the approach is made through an attic reached by a long flight of stairs. Mac-Donald himself wrote in a letter, 'I have a passion for stairs,' and our man with a smattering of Freud, who connected stairs with coition, could of course have a field-day with this as with many other of MacDonald's symbols. Anyhow these attics are the counterpart to the cellars in the former book and to the subterranean passages, especially those inside mountains, which are always appearing in Mac-Donald. Both sets of images represent things outside the compass of the normal reasoning mind: some admirers have claimed that MacDonald, like Ibsen, was one of the few people of his time to pay due attention to the Unconscious. Looking back instead of forward, one can find parallels in traditional mythology. Thus, in regard to the points of intersection of our world and other worlds, Alwyn and Brinley Rees point out in *Celtic Heritage* that 'boundaries between territories, like boundaries between years and between seasons, are lines along which the supernatural intrudes through the surface of existence'.

Psychologically, MacDonald is as rich as Spenser. He is also as moral as Spenser. But, unlike Kingsley, there is nothing facile about his morality. He sees that the problem of evil really *is* a problem. Thus in *Phantastes* he creates a macabre creature called the 'Alder Maiden' who, like Spenser's Duessa, leads or rather *is* a double life: the hero, who has fallen into her clutches from which he never fully recovers, is left reflecting: 'How can beauty and ugliness dwell so near?' There are similar false females in Malory and, more relevantly, in Shelley's *Epipsychidion* (see above, p. 63). Immediately after the encounter with the Alder Maiden, and partly because of it, the hero is saddled with something described as his 'shadow' which throws a blight on everything he meets. In *Lilith* we meet another and far greater Shadow who stands to the whole of humanity as the earlier shadow stood to the hero of Phantastes. He can be equated with Satan and he is closely in league with Lilith herself. The quality of this Shadow is suggested through a few subtle touches. Thus a small child says: 'He was all black through between us, and we could not see one another; and then he was inside us.' The effect on the children is to make them unlike themselves. Later, the hero of the book finds him blocking his path: 'I seemed to pass through him, but I think now that he passed through me: for a moment I was as one of the damned.' Lastly there is the comment made on him by Adam: 'Wretched creature, he has himself within himself, and cannot rest.' Yet Adam makes a saving qualification: 'Without a substance a shadow cannot be—yea, or without a light behind the substance!'

On a less cosmic scale MacDonald's moral view of the universe means that his heroes and heroines have to develop and they usually do it the hard way. MacDonald talks about Fairies and Fairy Land as freely as Barrie but in attitude as in vision he is poles apart from him: MacDonald would never tolerate Peter Pan or, for that matter, Wendy. There are indeed Peter Pan-like children in *Lilith* but the hero sees that their growth has been arrested and feels that it is his mission to cure this. MacDonald's heroes have not only to prove themselves through action, like Tom in *The Water Babies*, they have also to achieve a spiritual evolution. This involves paradoxes which are nearly all variants on the Christian paradox that one must lose one's life to save it. In *Lilith* when we first meet Adam he is in the form of a librarian, but he promptly turns into a raven and this raven is also a sexton, but a creative sexton. Thus he suddenly plunges his beak into the earth 'drawing out a great wriggling red worm. He threw back his head, and tossed it in the air. It spread great wings, gorgeous in red and black, and soared aloft.' The raven explains: 'When you have nothing to bury, you must dig something up!' In the next chapter he tells us: 'But indeed the business of the universe is to make such a fool of you that you will know yourself for one, and so begin to be wise!' And here I will leave MacDonald. In this particular kind of parable writing I think no one could go much further.

V

THE CONTEMPORARY WORLD:
POETRY AND DRAMA

I N the Victorian Age what I call 'parable writing' was better represented in children's books than in orthodox 'grown-up' poetry, drama or prose fiction. But this could not last: when we reach the twentieth century, children's fantasy is represented, I suppose, typically by *Peter Pan*, a work which is not only frivolous but perverse. So, now that we have come to our own time, we can leave children's books behind us and look for what parable writing we can find in the three main categories of verse, drama, and prose fiction. In each of these we have already considered some outstanding specimens from earlier periods: *The Faerie Queene*, *Everyman* and *Pilgrim's Progress*. All three of these are separated from us by one or more great gulfs, so great that we might not expect contemporary specimens to have anything much in common with them. And yet, I think, we may find contemporary works that have more in common with these illustrious predecessors than with much that has been written in the interval.

If this is so, we should not be too glib in assigning reasons for it; the evolution of literature in the twentieth century is a vastly complicated affair. But if it is true that the wheel of creative writing has moved round, though far from full circle, to a position more like that of Spenser, one of the reasons surely must be the growing dissatisfaction that many people feel with the sort of 'realistic' writing that is primarily concerned with man as seen in a supposedly objective way, in the conventional double framework of a recognizable external nature and some well-established human society: what E. M. Forster called 'the world of telegrams and anger'. Such literary realism rested upon wider optimistic assumptions, both about science and about human society, that had been made by most educated people since the early days of the Enlightenment till, say, the First World War. These assumptions had of course been challenged long before that, but only by a small if very varied minority. Enlightenment literature is essentially secular: in the nineteenth century a minority writer like George Mac-Donald, seeing that man cannot live by science alone, very naturally wrote, even in his more playful works, from a basically religious angle. And it was equally natural, for example, that Tolstoy, after his conversion, should have repudiated his own secular works and confined himself to writing from a specifically Christian angle. But in our time, while there are far more people in reaction against both the assumptions of the rationalist Enlightenment and the sort of realism these encourage in literature, there are far fewer people who can express such a reaction in traditional Christian terms: here at least Spenser and Bunyan and the author of *Everyman* remain on the other side of a great gulf. Whether, leaving Christianity out of it, most modern writers can write from a religious angle at all, is open to argument. Mr Esslin found a specifically religious element in writers like Samuel Beckett. And the family tree of Existentialism includes Kierkegaard. But it depends on what one means by religion: this will crop up again.

Now to consider the first of my three literary categories:

What about recent English parable writing in verse? I would say at once that, in any strict sense of the phrase 'parable writing', it is not to be compared with the output in prose or in the drama. One of the reasons for this is, quite simply, that the long poem or at any rate the long narrative poem has gone out of fashion. Another reason is that poets for the last few generations have been concerned with other things. Tennyson has long been dead, but it is still quite common for a poet to assume that he has done enough in the making of a poem if his descriptions of external objects —particularly visual descriptions of objects from natural history—are exact enough and attractive enough. Of course it is impossible to describe without doing more than describe. There will always be some wider reference and some degree of symbolism will creep in whether you know it or not and whether you wish it or not. But to have one's sights lowered to description as one's primary target certainly tends to preclude parable writing. The same is equally true, if not more so, of poets who confine themselves to neat comments on human behaviour as seen from the outside and even on their own behaviour as they *try* to see it from outside. There has been too much of this forced objectivity lately. We do still get a certain amount of lyric poetry in the narrower sense, but this, though it may admit, does not require, parable. Moreover, those poets of our time who would seem to be temperamentally predisposed to parable have generally gone in for a good deal of symbolism which contains a noticeable spine of allegory.

Take Mr Eliot for instance. Like most parabolists he is certainly concerned more with the inside of man than with his outside; the desert in *The Waste Land*, for example, is

as much an interior landscape as the forests in *The Faerie
Queene*. But Eliot's *method* is different. The Elizabethans,
as we noticed long since, regularly related allegory to
metaphor, allegory being thought of as extended metaphor
or metaphor as allegory in miniature. But Eliot is not a
great exploiter of metaphor; he still uses images more as
they were used by the Imagists, though for quite a different
purpose. In Imagism proper, as Graham Hough has
written, 'the image itself begins to acquire special value,
rather than the thing that it is the image of.... There is a
growing belief that all the work of literature is done by
images, not by syntax or dianoia.... There is a tendency
to regard images atomically and disjunctively, and the
longer poetic units try to make their effect by the juxta-
position of images—like *The Waste Land* or Pound's *Cantos*
—theme is only allowed to make its appearance surrepti-
tiously.' I do not myself find the theme in *The Waste Land*,
let alone the *Four Quartets*, all that surreptitious; but I do
agree that, while Eliot is a modest man, the images he uses
are arrogant, they think they are there in their own right.
Eliot has indulged them. He has himself written of the
almost magical compulsion exercised upon a poet by certain
remembered objects or events in his own experience: their
significance is something he cannot explain, but he *feels* it.
An example in his own work comes in 'The Journey of the
Magi':

> And an old white horse galloped away in the meadow.
> Then we came to a tavern with vine-leaves over the lintel,
> Six hands at an open door dicing for pieces of silver.

As metaphor, or even as symbol, these gamblers and that
old horse have nothing to do with the Magi. They are there,

it would seem, as decoration or, at the most, as props: we appear to be back on the level of Tennyson, but without Tennyson's flair for detail. But in fact, as most readers feel, we are not back on that level at all. These images are significant; but why, they cannot say, any more than their author can. Perhaps this is another instance of C. S. Lewis's 'sacramentalism'; but, whatever it is, it has no place in my category of 'parable writing'.

W. H. Auden is another *anima naturaliter parabolica*, but he also strays off along roads similar to Eliot's: as he would admit himself, his poems are full of 'sacred objects'; but, more often than not, this means that they are sacred to him as a private individual and for reasons which may be mainly accidental (e.g. the landscapes—Midland slag heaps, Cornish tin mines and so on—which he happened to meet as a child). From the first he has been very ready to use a sampling system, a kind of synecdoche, the part standing for the whole: hence in his early poems the continual use of pioneers, mountaineers, engineers, scouts, spies, and so on as types of the advance guard of contemporary humanity— or sometimes just types of humanity. Like Spenser and Bunyan, he also draws freely on an accumulated reservoir of images, fed as much from the nursery as from the library, e.g. certain nightmare figures that might come out of Struwwelpeter:

> the hooded women, the humpbacked surgeons
> And the Scissor Man.

Unlike Eliot, Auden makes much use of metaphor but there is something atomic in *his* method too. If at times he is a parabolist, he is not a consistent or sustained one. Thus his long poem, *The Age of Anxiety*, proceeds throughout on the verge of parable: there are four characters who share their fantasies with us—and sometimes with each other—but the content of these fantasies is largely arbitrary. To put it another way, here again this poet, like the more obviously descriptive type of poet, is getting his effects by enumeration rather than by fusion. Among the poets of our time in English there are few pure examples of the parabolist. One such is the late Edwin Muir whom I shall come back to. I will only say here that, though he is much to be admired for his consistency both of aim and method, I find it refreshing, after reading him at length, to return from him to the impurities of Auden.

Before leaving the subject of verse, I want to look back at three earlier poems which may serve as a better bridge between the works I discussed in the previous chapter and those I am coming to. Only one of these three could properly be called an allegory, so, disregarding chronology, I will take it first. I mean that famous or notorious poem, *The Hound of Heaven* by Francis Thompson. The first stanza begins:

> I fled Him, down the nights and down the days;
> I fled Him, down the arches of the years;
> I fled Him, down the labyrinthine ways
> Of my own mind . . .

Note the Shelleyesque phrase 'the arches of the years' and the Shelleyesque epithet 'labyrinthine'. Thompson was as egocentric as Shelley, though with, one might say, less to be egocentric about. This poem is not, however, in my opinion as bad as most modern critics would have it. The Hound of Heaven is of course God, and the piece as a whole is a genuine devotional outpouring. But it is a very uneven poem, not living up to its beginning, and suffers from technical flaws and lapses of taste. Or, as so often, one can invert the criticism and say: Thompson's complex of belief, experience and attitude is of an inferior kind that predisposes him to just such flaws and lapses. The poem deteriorates about halfway through, where the rhythmical pattern changes: there is far too much highfalutin, overdone diction, and in general too much writing that is out of key. As just one example of a bad image, what about 'The pulp so bitter, how shall taste the rind?' Surely, when one eats a fruit, the rind is the first thing one meets. More serious than this, the sequence of images is so random that the whole resembles one great mixed metaphor, while the basic hound image, having been dropped for forty lines, is picked up again too abruptly and with a very awkward rhyme:

> Now of that long pursuit
> Comes on at hand the bruit.

I would not have brought in this embarrassing and to me unsympathetic poem, if it had not been one of the last obvious Christian allegories in English verse. I would hazard a paradox here; if Thompson had not been, in the vulgar sense, such an 'unworldly' or 'other-worldly' person, he would probably have been better equipped to put over the claims of the other world. If we now for contrast go back to an earlier generation, having already severely criticised Christina Rossetti's verse allegories, I may make some amends by mentioning a very fine poem by her brother Dante Gabriel Rossetti. It is a poem often found in anthologies and is called 'The Woodspurge'.

> The wind flapped loose, the wind was still,
> Shaken out dead from tree and hill:

I had walk'd on at the wind's will—
I sat now, for the wind was still.

Between my knees my forehead was—
My lips, drawn in, said not Alas!
My hair was over in the grass,
My naked ears heard the day pass.

My eyes, wide open, had the run
Of some ten weeds to fix upon;
Among those few, out of the sun,
The woodspurge flower'd, three cups in one.

From perfect grief there need not be
Wisdom or even memory:
One thing learnt remains to me—
The woodspurge has a cup of three.

Lovers of peripheral suggestion and of the further-flung types of ambiguity can make what they like of the 'cup of three'. The point about this poem is that it achieves something positive (the portrayal of 'perfect grief') by sparsity, elimination, negation. The wind that no longer blows, the lips that do *not* say Alas, the eyes that do *not* close and yet do not look at anything except one tiny patch of ground, these within the small scale of the poem, and combined with the excellently muted versification, achieve a marriage of form and content which in Francis Thompson was precluded by inadequacies of one or the other or, more likely, of both. Whether it is correct or not to call 'The Woodspurge' a piece of parable writing, it is certainly not just realism, not a merely descriptive or documentary poem. The woodspurge itself, seen in close-up and from above, has the significance, however inexplicable, of those images that Eliot mentions, such as the 'old white horse', or those images in all our dreams which look very ordinary and not particularly relevant and yet click with something inside us.

My third verse specimen is very different from both the other two. We must come forward again in time to A. E. Housman, a peculiar, limited, but underrated poet with whom any history of modern English poetry might very well start. An excessive preoccupation on our part with technique or with what used to be called 'experiment' blinded us, I think, to certain important similarities between Housman and Eliot. Apart from anything else, both are imbued with classical standards, yet both are belated Romantics. Housman, unlike Eliot, is usually a lucid poet but the poem below is one of his few obscure ones, being capable of different interpretations; it is also one of the very few—'Hell Gate' is possibly another and so is the one about Lot's wife—that could conceivably be classed as 'allegorical'. A personal reason for quoting it here is that it gave me the idea for an unsuccessful radio play about which I shall shortly say a few words. But first, the poem:

> Her strong enchantments failing,
>   Her towers of fear in wreck,
> Her limbecks dried of poisons
>   And the knife at her neck,
>
> The Queen of air and darkness
>   Begins to shrill and cry:
> 'O young man, O my slayer,
>   Tomorrow you shall die.'
>
> O Queen of air and darkness,
>   I think 'tis truth you say,
> And I shall die tomorrow;
>   But you will die today.

We must not be put off by the hymn-tune metre since, often in Housman, when he is expressing something especially sombre, sadly fatalistic or near-nihilistic, the patness of the metre is an essential irony. As to the symbolism of this poem, I am far from sure what Housman precisely meant by it, that is, if he meant anything by it *precisely*. But the phrase 'air and darkness' at once places the mysterious figure of its queen in the same traditional category as Goethe's Mephistopheles, only here it is rather as if Mephistopheles had coalesced with Helen: or again we could compare MacDonald's figure of Lilith. The experience anyhow is literally a disenchantment: the revolt against some almost cosmic Untruth to which the young man had been a slave, although this slavery possibly enabled him to go on living. It is typical of Housman that he imposes this double-edged liberation on his young man while he is young. One can correlate this poem with his many poems about suicide, where the person concerned is never of unsound mind.

Whether Housman's poem can be called allegorical or not, it gave me, as I said, the idea for a radio play which is one of the few things I have written where I deliberately attempted allegory. Conceivably my experience, though unsatisfactory, may throw a little light on how allegory *can* be written—or possibly on how it should *not* be written. To start with my source, the Housman poem, I excerpted from it what I wanted—the figures of the Queen and the Young Man and their tit-for-tat about dying tomorrow and today—then expanded this as I wanted in a particular direction. Without bothering about Housman's intentions, I made the Queen the source of the sort of perverted idealism which inspired, for instance, Hitler. My hero, who became a dictator, was accordingly a self-deceiver: what the Queen had really given him was the lust for power. When I came to embody this central idea in the actual play I found that two things happened: symbols began to proliferate and the Queen herself began to turn into a person—a tragic person. As I set her outside ordinary time and place, I found myself confronted with the same sort of problem that George MacDonald was always tackling, though I suspect his solutions were usually 'given' to him: thus the Queen stood to my hero very much as, in MacDonald, Lilith stands to the hero Mr Vane. But my superstructure was less convincing than MacDonald's because I lacked his ground-work of belief. As for my supporting symbols, they hap-pened; I did not usually look for them. The Queen had to work on her victims, those she doomed to become her lovers, from a distance; possibly some half-conscious memory of the Lady of Shalott made me supply her with a magic mirror which showed, very much like a television set, scenes taking place in the world of human beings. Out of these she picked her next victim. As this play was getting itself written, I realized that the most difficult scene would be the final confrontation and struggle to the death between the Queen and this lover who has never seen her. For in killing her he will, so far as the allegory goes, be killing something in himself, whereas, so far as the drama goes, it takes two persons, not one, to make a struggle. This is the kind of dilemma which is often latent in *The Faerie Queene*. Thus, to take one example, it can be argued that the terrible enchanter Busirane, who carries off Amoret on the day of her wedding to Scudamour and proceeds to imprison and torture her, is himself a sort of hypostatized other-side-of-the-medal, a flaking-off or distorted reflection of the love between Amoret and Scudamour. If this is so, Spenser certainly had the knack of making such reflections solid or, putting it more generally, of making his abstractions concrete. It is a knack I envy him.

As regards plays, I shall be returning shortly to that 'Theatre of the Absurd' celebrated by Mr Esslin. Esslin's favourite playwrights, such as Beckett and Pinter, do not as a rule admit to having allegorical intentions, and their critics more often than not find that any one character or situation or occurrence in these plays has not merely a double meaning but a whole sheaf of meanings: think of the relationship of Pozzo and Lucky in *Waiting for Godot* or the ever-growing corpse in Ionesco's play *Amédée*. But first let us look back to an older playwright who has already been admitted as a parabolist by many critics and who is still, I think, a great—and useful—influence among us. I mean Ibsen, and not only the author of *Peer Gynt* but also of the later prose plays. *Peer Gynt* has been bracketed with Goethe's *Faust* by Northrop Frye as an example of 'free-style allegory'. Like some plays by Beckett and other modern playwrights, it hinges on the question of identity, 'the Gyntian self'. It is this question that precipitates most of the more obviously allegorical scenes, with the Boyg, the Trolls, and, above all, the Button Moulder. In act III, scene 3, which is the turning-point of the play, the allegory scores its most palpable hit. The outlawed and self-tortured Peer has just finished building his hut in the forest when, to his astonishment and delight, he is joined by Solveig who announces she has come to live with him: 'Here,' she says,

'I am at home.' She goes into the hut but, before Peer can follow her, a horrible couple appear with horrible promptitude. It is his old troll-bride with an ugly limping boy who, she tells Peer, is his son. 'We're neighbours,' she says. 'Are we?' says Peer, 'That's news to me.' To which she makes the devastating reply: 'As your hut was built, mine rose at its side.' This impingement of his past upon his future is what finishes Peer, though the play is not yet halfway through. The haunting menace of the Troll Woman—

I'll be at your side in my rightful place.
We'll share you. We'll take it in turns in your bed—

is very similar to the haunting menace of the corpse in Ionesco that keeps growing in the next room till its legs break through into the sitting-room.

Ibsen never again wrote anything like *Peer Gynt*; but it is a mistake to think that in his later plays he was consistently a realist whose main concern was social problems, or at least conflicts between people treated objectively. He seems quite as much concerned with the insides of people who, whatever their position in the community, remain, like Peer Gynt, isolated individuals. In certain plays, moreover, in order to achieve a greater depth than is possible through sheer realism, he starts relying upon symbols. He himself spoke of using a 'new method' in *The Wild Duck*, and his recent translator, Mr Michael Meyer, writes that here we have 'a single and precise symbol' which is 'the hub and heart' of the play: it is, he goes on, 'as though the wild duck were a magnet and the characters in the play so many iron filings held together by this centripetal force'. Similarly, Dr John Northam in *Ibsen's Dramatic Method* (1953) stresses the significance of Ibsen's stage directions in this play. The sliding doors in the back wall can open to reveal an attic which, says Northam, is 'both a symbol of protective phantasy and a real attic containing real animals'. He also makes much of the net and the sail-cloth which at one point are draped across the opening to the attic. In *The Wild Duck*, according to Northam, 'the symbol is, for the first time [he is talking, of course, only of the prose plays], a physical reality on the stage, or near enough for it to suggest actual presence'. It seems to me that Ibsen, both in this symbolical use of stage properties and in his more general insinuation of symbolism into what purports to be a realistic play, is very much akin to those of our contemporary parabolists, like Pinter, who convey their parables by sleight-of-hand or throw-away. The method of *The Wild Duck*, it would seem, has 'dated' less than that of *Peer Gynt*.

Something parallel is true in the history of recent prose fiction, where for this kind of writing Kafka seems to be the prototype. I shall, however, say a little here about one prose book which, though published in 1927, three years after Kafka's death, yet, superficially anyhow, seems to belong to an earlier period, earlier even than *The Wild Duck*. It has something in common with the Button Moulder scenes in *Peer Gynt*, and also with some of the children's fantasies I have discussed, though the special world it presents is not, in the conventional phrase, very 'suitable for children'. I mean *Mr Weston's Good Wine* by T. F. Powys. This curious book definitely *is* an allegory and of an old-fashioned kind. T. F. Powys is as much concerned as George MacDonald with love, death and eternity, and more concerned than he is with lust, greed, brutality, spite, envy and sheer crass hatred. One of the characters in this book, an innocent who preaches to the animals, is found at one point reading from William Law's *A Serious Call to a Devout and Holy Life* the sentence: 'But do not be affected at these things, the world is a great dream, and few people are awake in it.' This, which might serve as a text for *Mr Weston's Good Wine*, is again reminiscent of MacDonald; but Powys chooses a very different setting for his inter-meddling of two worlds. He invents an Olde English Village, where the locals have names like Mumby, Bunce, Meek and Grunter: the focal point of this village is an oak tree overshadowing what is called 'the oak tree bed' in which the young bloods ravish the village belles. Into this narrow and complacent society Powys brings God in the shape of a travelling tradesman, cosy, tweedy, humorous, and also a little vain and at moments a little regretful. This quaintly disguised God (a god of Biblical origin) is presented with touches of irony or word-play: 'And, although entirely self-taught—for he had risen, as so many important people do, from nothing—he had read much, and had written too.' He is accompanied by a beautiful young man, who appears to be the Archangel Michael; this Michael gets the vicar's daughter into the oak tree bed, after which she ascends to heaven. But the central and catalytic image in this story is the wine itself which Mr Weston sells. His ordinary wine illuminates and makes people love one another, but he has a special vintage wine which represents death: 'Yes,' said Mr Weston, 'we allow no credit for that wine.' The most imaginative touch in the book is perhaps when Mr Weston is asked if he will ever drink this special vintage himself. 'The day will come when I hope to drink of it,' replied Mr Weston gravely.

To attempt a précis of the whole story for those who have not read it would only suggest an implausible whimsicality, tainted here and there with voyeurism, sadism and necrophily. But, in fact, T. F. Powys is a true descendant of Bunyan (though also perhaps a spiritual cousin of D. H. Lawrence) and the fantasy works because he has the innocence of his convictions. The self-imposed convention of *Mr Weston* works better than, for instance, that of a comparable book in the same period, *War in Heaven* by Charles Williams. Powys has had, so far as I know, no direct successors in England; but William Golding, for one, was dealing in his first three novels with similar simplified worlds constructed on parallel lines. As Mr John Wain has written of Golding, 'he believes in the existence of cruelty and savagery and also in the existence of sainthood and redemption. His ultimate terms of reference are religious, indeed specifically Christian.' From the murderous boys of *The Lord of the Flies* and the innocent and inarticulate Neanderthal men of *The Inheritors* it is not such a far step to the suffering old tramps and invalids and cripples and near-halfwits of Samuel Beckett. And Beckett too has been described as a religious writer.

Beckett himself has denied that Godot stands for God; Godot is no Mr Weston nor is he a Hound of Heaven tha refused to come to heel. Yet Esslin's statement that *Waiting for Godot* is 'concerned with the hope of salvation through the workings of grace' makes sense if we remember his other statement that 'the subject of the play is not Godot but waiting, the act of waiting as an essential and characteristic aspect of the human condition'. Many critics, similarly, are agreed that another work, which is also a story of waiting and frustration, is also concerned with what Christians call the 'action of grace': I mean Kafka's novel *The Castle*. It looks as if in these two works, as in many others of our time, there is an underlying paradoxical riddle: When is unbelief *not* unbelief? Beckett has said: 'I am interested in the shape of ideas even if I do not believe in them.' Now a playwright, like a poet, being a maker (or 'makar') is thereby *ipso facto* a shaper (this is true however much he may dispense with plot, metre, etc.), and this very act of shaping may bring him back full circle into something very like belief—rather as if God in the first chapter of Genesis, when he looked at his work and saw that it was good, had found himself forced to believe in himself. Perhaps a better analogy could be found in the third chapter of Genesis, where God's creatures by disobeying him force him again to take action, even though this time it is punitive action; in a way this is both to his credit and to theirs.

We seem here to be getting dangerously near to that anti-philosophy, Existentialism. Beckett, I understand, has denied that he is an Existentialist; but I would tentatively suggest that, just as Yeats admitted that the point of his scheme in 'A Vision' was to give him a scaffolding for his poetry, so conceivably the main function of Existentialism is to enable Existentialists to write plays and novels. Working backwards then, as from the creation to the creator, Beckett, I suggest, could be called an Existentialist not *de jure* but *de facto*. I have already mentioned one of Beckett's favourite quotations: 'Nothing is more real than nothing.' 'Nothing', in this mystical sense, seems to be an essential part of the foundations of religion. Thus George MacDonald in *Lilith* described Lilith during her final struggle when 'the source of life had withdrawn itself': 'She was what God could not have created. She had usurped beyond her share in self-creation, and her part had undone His! . . . Her right hand also was now clenched—upon existent Nothing—her inheritance!' For all this dissimilarity in kind and calibre Beckett and MacDonald seem to me nearer to each other, both in their mythopoeia and in whatever underlies and inspires their mythopoeia, than either of them is, say, to Bertolt Brecht. And in this sense at least I would agree that Beckett is a religious writer. This would again support one of my basic contentions—that a religious theme, when it gets into literature, requires some sort of parable form.

Often, as we have seen, the parable takes the guise of a quest, and either *Waiting for Godot* or *Endgame* could be described, if paradoxically, as a *static* quest. But why this contradiction in terms? Esslin suggests an answer. Beckett, he says, is working 'at a level where neither characters nor plot exist. Characters presuppose that human nature, the diversity of personality and individuality, is real and matters; plot can exist only on the assumption that events in time are significant.' He accordingly compares Beckett's characters to 'the personified virtues and vices in medieval mystery plays', which are dealing not with events as such but with 'types of *situation* that will forever repeat themselves'. This is why *Godot* has two acts: it could have had a hundred and two but it could not have had one. And, if events in time are out, so is discursive thinking. 'Beckett's entire work', writes Esslin, 'can be seen as a search for the reality that lies behind mere reasoning in conceptual terms.' This purging—one might almost say this liquidation—of content is found by him to be reflected in Beckett's use of language. 'Language', he says, 'in Beckett's plays serves to express the breakdown, the disintegration of language.'

As I said at the outset, I think Esslin overstates this. Beckett is a master conjurer, and Esslin has perhaps been deceived by the trick—those white rabbits do seem to have vanished but they have not *disintegrated*, they were, and are, real rabbits. In the same way Esslin writes: 'The dialogue in Beckett's plays is often built on the principle that each line obliterates what was said in the previous line.' This is perceptive but one should not give too much weight to the word 'obliterates'. Just as in a simple 'Tu quoque' slanging match one party can never obliterate the other, so Beckett's dialogue, like the theme which inspires it, is essentially dialectical. We can compare with it much of the dialogue in Kafka and also the self-communings of his heroes; these too show the same nagging concern with truth. We can also compare, *mutatis mutandis*, the dialogue in Lewis Carroll's Alice books. This comparison with Alice is not frivolous: Esslin subtitles his chapter on Beckett 'The Search for the Self', and that is just what Alice is searching for much of the time both in *Wonderland* and in *Through the Looking-Glass*. Beckett also uses many of the same tricks as Lewis Carroll—the kinky logic, the word-play and so on. I will give one very short example from *Endgame*. Hamm, the blind old ruler, and Clov, his hopeless slave, are conversing in their claustrophobic room in a world which seems to have been left over from an apocalypse.

HAMM (*speaks first*): Clov!
CLOV: Yes.
HAMM: Nature has forgotten us.

CLOV: There's no more nature.
HAMM: No more nature! You exaggerate.
CLOV: In the vicinity.
HAMM: But we breathe, we change!
We lose our hair, our teeth! Our bloom!
Our ideals!
CLOV: Then she hasn't forgotten us.
HAMM: But you say there is none.
CLOV (*sadly*): No one that ever lived ever thought so
crooked as we.

The comparison with Alice may also remind us that Beckett is a very funny writer. We have often noticed how specialists in parable writing tend to bolster up their special worlds by means of humour, wit, a matter-of-fact manner, a down-to-earth style, and the counterfeiting—sometimes the parodying—of common sense or logic or both.

Esslin includes among his playwrights of the Absurd N. F. Simpson, who is very close in method to Lewis Carroll—indeed in *One Way Pendulum* the mock trial inevitably reminds one of the trial in *Alice in Wonderland*. But, unlike most of the parabolists I have discussed, Simpson seems primarily concerned with the contemporary society in which he lives and with the surface of it at that: his parody therefore tends to be parody for its own sake and not a means to an end. But another very funny playwright can be properly bracketed with Beckett, namely Harold Pinter, who stands about halfway between Beckett and Simpson. He is more concerned with society, or with man in society, than Beckett: thus the mysterious menace in plays like *The Dumb Waiter* and *The Birthday Party* can, viewed from one angle, be regarded as typifying the menaces of our time, whether they come from the anarchic, violent side of society or from the conformist, bureaucratic or custom-ridden, suffocating side. Thus Esslin writes of *The Birthday Party* that it 'has been interpreted as an allegory of the pressures of conformity. . . . Yet the play can equally well be seen as an allegory of death.' This constitutional ambiguity—or double-level writing—is something that is often found today among poets. But those readers who have had too much of it and would write it off as a typical modern disease should remember that Spenser often practised something of the sort.

Among prose writers Pinter, in using this sort of ambiguity, had obviously one great predecessor in Kafka. Thus *The Castle*, as I said, has been considered by many to be about the changes in a soul brought about through the action of grace. This may well be so, but it does not invalidate those other admirers of Kafka who ask, like Mr Goronwy Rees: 'What else is *The Castle* but a Zionist epic of that people's [the Jewish people's] effort to found a community and a home?' But just as those of us who like a simple and single interpretation are about to applaud this rhetorical question, Mr Rees himself raps us over the knuckles: 'The answer to such questions', he continues, 'is, of course, that *The Trial* and *The Castle* are much else besides.' A few pages further on in the same book Kafka's great friend, Max Brod, stresses the autobiographical element in *The Castle*, which 'reflects,' he says, 'in a distorted form, Kafka's love affair with Milena [Milena Jesenska], described with a curious scepticism and prejudice which perhaps offered Kafka his only way out of the crisis'. In this quite acceptable working of several levels at once or, if you prefer it, this successful blending of several apparently disparate, if parallel, themes, Pinter is one of Kafka's natural heirs. There have been several false claimants to the heritage and nothing is more tedious than a bad imitation of Kafka.

I started by calling Pinter a funny writer. The best comment on this comes from Pinter himself in a letter to *The Sunday Times* (14 August 1960): 'As far as I'm concerned *The Caretaker* is funny up to a point. Beyond that point it ceases to be funny, and it was because of that point that I wrote it.' In an interview he added that his characters are discovered 'at the extreme edge of their living, where they are living pretty much alone'. This brings us back to Beckett, whose characters are always 'at the extreme edge of their living'. Yet this does not mean that the plays of either Pinter or Beckett are portrayals of solipsism, for even failed interdependence, as in *The Caretaker*, implies the virtues of interdependence. As for the sordid or morbid side of Beckett, the compulsive dwelling upon physical decay, or excretion, or upon sex reduced to a tragicomic and nightmarish yet tedious absurdity, this comes from his basic single-mindedness. If you're stripping to the bone you must strip through the bowels first. It is part of the search for truth—or identity—and necessary to Beckett's catharsis.

Esslin, I think, in his eulogy of these playwrights, and of others such as Ionesco and Genêt, falls into a fallacy when he writes that they are concerned with 'man stripped of the accidental circumstances of social position or historical context'. The same could have been said almost as plausibly of *Everyman* or of *Pilgrim's Progress*; but in none of these cases is it more than comparatively true. Everyman remains a man of the Middle Ages and Christian a man of the seventeenth century. I suspect further that Christian has a Bedford accent just as the tramps in *Godot*, even when they are speaking French, have an Irish one. More seriously, the attitudes expressed in these plays belong very much to our period. But Esslin's more important point is true: that a writer like Beckett is essentially lyrical, a great deal more so than the ordinary run of playwrights. He is concerned, as Esslin says, with the 'quest for the answer to such basic questions as "Who am I?"' This is the sort of question that used to be the prerogative of poets. One great twentieth-century poet who in his later work was mainly concerned with such problems was Rilke. The questions put by poets like Rilke admit of no answer: the nearest one gets to an answer is in the sheer phrasing of the question. And even that phrasing involves the sort of juggling with tokens that the mystics are driven to when they try to describe their experiences. Even Beckett, in comparison with Rilke, has his feet on the earth; and so have his characters compared with what Rilke calls 'angels'. For Beckett after all, though a static playwright, remains a playwright. Lyrical though he may be, he also remains in line with those parabolists I have already discussed who used narrative prose or verse or wrote plays in prose or verse.

I shall end this chapter by considering a lyrical poet of our time who expresses his view of the universe almost entirely through forms of parable. I mean Edwin Muir. Muir was so consistent in his aims, which merge into a single aim, and his metaphysico-mystical writing is so unadulterated either by topical or documentary elements or by primarily aesthetic ones, such as images used for their own sake, that I find reading many of his poems on end is like walking through a gallery of abstract paintings. Like MacDonald he is concerned with the interpenetration of time and what I suppose we must call Eternity, but unlike MacDonald he cannot embody these in genuinely concrete images, let alone stories or characters. He uses images drawn from landscape and fauna but these tend to approx-imate to what Mr Hough calls 'hieratic emblems'. His lions and horses are flat and heraldic and indeed are some-times described in terms of heraldry. Some of his poems are narrative but yet there is no movement in them. We may compare the static quests of Beckett, but at least in his plays (I am not so happy about his prose) there is usually more than one voice.

In spite of all this, Muir is an important poet. In his volume of short poems, *Journeys and Places* (1937), the journeys and places are all metaphorical. The method remains the same in all the succeeding volumes. What he has to say is always deeply felt, but his way of saying it is only sometimes either arresting or memorable. His more successful poems seem to me to be those which achieve the kind of dream quality we have met in Spenser and Mac-Donald, among others. Such poems are 'The Hill', in *Journeys and Places*, and in the next volume the title poem 'The Narrow Place' and a poem called 'Then', built on a central nightmarish image of

> angry shadows fighting on a wall
> That now and then sent out a groan
> Buried in lime and stone,
> And sweated now and then like tortured wood
> Big drops that looked yet did not look like blood.

Like MacDonald, Muir is continually concerned with the relations of evil to good. In a poem called 'The Three Mirrors', the second stanza ends:

> The crack ran over the floor,
> The child at peace in his play
> Changed as he passed through a door,
> Changed were the house and the tree,
> Changed the dead in the knoll,
> For locked in love and grief
> Good with evil lay.

But the third stanza suggests a reconciliation or redemption. It begins:

> If I looked in the third glass
> I should see evil and good
> Standing side by side
> In the ever standing wood,
> The wise king safe on his throne . . .

This is a quite usual view among mystics but it does not make for drama or a good story. MacDonald, in *Lilith* for example, arranges the redemption of Lilith herself and appears to hint at the possibility of the redemption of the Shadow, i.e. Satan, but this will lie outside the story. To be fair, Muir in 'The Three Mirrors' does begin his third stanza with an 'If', so this static happy ending where each is going to be

> so deeply grown
> Into his own place
> He'd be past desire or doubt

does lie outside the story too.

I prefer those poems of Muir where all the evils have not yet been exorcized. Thus in the title poem of *The Labyrinth*

(1949) the hero (Theseus adapted for metaphor) has long since killed the bull and got back into the world and yet

> since I came out that day
> There have been times when I have heard my footsteps
> Still echoing in the maze.

Like the bemused characters in Beckett or Kafka, the hero of this poem sometimes fears that the labyrinth is chasing him. Or else his bad spirit sneers:

> 'No, do not hurry.
> No need to hurry. Haste and delay are equal
> In this one world, for there's no exit, none,
> No place to come to, and you'll end where you are,
> Deep in the centre of the endless maze.'

Opposed to this lying world of the labyrinth is the (allegedly) 'real world' of the gods, the belief in which is the hero's mainstay. But Muir here concludes by not forcing the conclusion:

> Oh these deceits are strong almost as life.
> Last night I dreamt I was in the labyrinth,
> And woke far on. I did not know the place.

You have probably, even in these short excerpts, noticed the flatness of the versification. This seems appropriate to the bleakness of the content. Yet what lies beneath or beyond that content was obviously not bleak at all. Muir too had known the Delectable Mountains. Among the parable writers of our time he stands as a foil to those who find the centre in Angst.

THE CONTEMPORARY WORLD:
PROSE NARRATIVE

For it is all very well to keep silence, but one has also
to consider the kind of silence one keeps.

THIS quotation comes from *The Unnamable*, a novel
(or imaginative work in prose) by Samuel Beckett,
which the French, I am told, call *The Unreadable*.
It seemed an apposite opening for my last chapter on the
elusive subject of parable, which has become more elusive
and more paradoxical as we approached our own time.
Samuel Beckett in his plays has probably made more use
of silence than any playwright before him. Martin Esslin
would attribute this to an attempt to express the Ineffable:
the Theatre of the Absurd, he writes, 'tends toward a
radical devaluation of language, toward a poetry that is to
emerge from the concrete and objectified images of the stage
itself'. This seems to imply that the set and props of
Endgame—the two little high windows that can only be
reached by a step-ladder, the picture turned with its face
to the wall, the single armchair on castors and the three-
legged stuffed dog—are as important in this play as the
dialogue. Perhaps they are, though I doubt it. But
Beckett elsewhere has produced a play without words, to be
mimed by a single actor, a symbolic and highly typical study
of frustration, and in all his plays both the mime element
and the frozen pauses ('those unheard are deeper') do bulk
large. In a play of the same kind, *The Chairs* by Ionesco, the

chairs themselves, which eventually fill the stage and on which no one ever sits, pull the full weight of characters. But Beckett began as a novelist and still continues to turn out long works of prose. Here, as in my opening quotation, when he means silence he has to *talk* about it. I will not say this puts him in a paradoxical position since that seems to be the position in which he started. I will merely point out that this is a characteristic paradox not only of Beckett but of our time. Beckett himself seems to have gone as far as is possible for a prose writer in presenting this paradox free of adulterating elements. Beyond this point a writer must stop writing and become a Carthusian or a Carmelite. Other prose writers of our time have included some of the adulterating elements, and have found them perhaps not so adulterating. But looking at a few specimens of this highly specialized prose fiction, I feel I should once again look back on the ground I have covered.

My last chapter provoked the question 'But can you think of a literary work that is *not* in some sense a parable?' My questioner himself suggested that Trollope might qualify. We are here near the root problem of what literature is about, but I would refer once again to the chapter on Allegory in *A Preface to the Faerie Queene* by Graham Hough. Mr Hough puts the simplest form of allegory, naïve allegory, at the opposite pole to what he calls 'realism', i.e. in his own words, 'plain, straightforward, univocal mimesis, innocent as far as may be of conceptual or typical suggestion altogether'. In practice, both these extremes tend to be a bore, but while the late Middle Ages suffered more from the former it is the latter from which we have suffered more in our time. Reporting proper, as practised by expert journalists, has nowadays reached a very high level, but the bulk of it, by its nature, is ephemeral. Sometimes, indeed, the nature of the subject-matter earns it a niche in the archives: it can become social or military history. But history is not—or at any rate should not be—creative writing, and what I deplore in our time is the excessive production of slices or chunks of life that pretend to be creative writing. Sometimes, as often in the 1930's and in certain novels today which deal with the working classes in midland or northern England, the sheer limitation of the content is taken to confer significance. This significance, unfortunately, is more often than not a label tacked on from outside rather than a light shining from within. At the same time we must admit that any novelist who has the gift of observation must find it almost impossible to confine himself to reporting his observations; if only because he must use selection, some genuine significance will creep in despite him. 'I am a camera' is not a good starting-point for an artist. Someone will say, 'But the camera also selects.' Of course it does not; it is the mind of its user that selects. But there *have* been in our time too many writers setting out to be cameras and nothing more.

In answer to the question 'Can you think of any literary work that is not in some sense a parable?' one has to recognize that nearly all 'realistic' fiction must be so, in however slight a sense. It is not just that anyone with ingenuity can read almost any sort of allegorical significance into anything (the ancients excelled in doing this both with Homer and with the Bible). That may be a very good parlour game but, so far as art is concerned, it is a perversion. There are, however, two reasons why all fiction is to some extent parabolical. One is the extremely artificial nature of language which, from the start, prevents a writer becoming a camera. The other is the simple fact that, when a novelist invents a character or situation or occurrence, these, if they are recognized at all by the reader as having anything to do with his own experience (and I take 'experience' here to include potential experience), will at once acquire a wider reference. They will stand for something not themselves; in other words, they will be symbols. So the difference between 'realistic writing' and 'parable writing' appears to be one of degree. But the difference in degree can be so vast that, as in many other spheres, it is convenient to use a rule of thumb and treat a really noticeable difference in degree as constituting a difference in kind. It is on this basis that I have tried to limit the subject-matter of the present book. Many may think that I have not limited it enough and that it is absurd to group together Spenser, Blake, Ibsen, Hans Andersen, Lewis Carroll, Samuel Beckett, Edwin Muir and William Golding, to mention only a few. But if you compare any of this group with any ordinary 'realistic' writer, you will see, I think, that in comparison with such realists the members of my group can helpfully be considered as being of the same kind.

Let me pick up some general points from my earlier chapters. In my first I explained why, *faute de mieux*, I had chosen the word 'parable'. But, having committed myself to this word, I see now that I have made a grave omission. I have hardly mentioned one important species of writing which obviously fits the name 'parable': I mean the didactic or propagandist fable or satirical fantasy, which has been so well represented in this country from *Gulliver* to *Animal*

Farm. I made this omission partly from lack of space but more, I think, because these works are primarily rationalist, which is not the case with the members of my group. And my group seemed wide enough already without bringing in this quite different species. Another question about grouping is suggested by Esslin's complaint that the French Existentialists 'express the new content in the old convention'. Esslin here, I think, goes too far. Sartre's play, *Huis Clos*, is a rationally constructed parable but its construction serves admirably to put over what Esslin calls 'the new content'. *Subjective* reality often finds literary expression in some sort of dream world—and indeed the hell of *Huis Clos* is very much of a dream hell—but many of the writers I have discussed do manage to present such worlds in a coherent and apparently logical manner: thus in the work as a whole we often get a strong story line, while in detail we have often found a plain and lucid style, a matter-of-fact tone, naturalistic dialogue and so on. Esslin sees that today writers have a renewed impulse to tackle the more mysterious aspects of human life, but he seems to assume that these can only be tackled by a technique of fragmentation or deliberate incoherence. Of the two living writers I shall discuss in this last chapter, Beckett does—with qualifications—employ such a technique; William Golding emphatically does not. But first I will go back to one of our great forerunners, Kafka.

Kafka is an extreme case. It would have been interesting, if time had permitted, to take for comparison some more normal-looking novels where the parable element is present but more or less disguised. In spite of surface differences, these might be found to have surprisingly much in common with Kafka. For example, one characteristic of Kafka's writings is claustrophobia, so it is easy to align with these the many modern novels that deal with closed communities. A very striking instance is *The Magic Mountain* by Thomas Mann, where a T.B. sanatorium appears, to borrow a phrase from T. S. Eliot, 'impatient to assume the world'. Among recent English examples one might cite *The Bell* by Iris Murdoch: here we not only have—an example of synecdoche, if you like that term—a religious lay community standing for the whole self-strangulating modern world, but also a central image which, as in *The Wild Duck* and *The Seagull*, acts as a magnet to which the characters are so many iron filings. Muriel Spark's novels are perhaps examples of the same kind of synecdoche; and, so far as the drama is concerned, no one has gone further in the closed community line than Eugene O'Neill in *The Iceman Cometh*. But Kafka to me seems not only more specialist but more universal than all these. His subject really is Everyman though it is Everyman very much in a twentieth-century context: some go further and say it is Everyman in the context of the Jewish quarter in Prague at the time Kafka was living there.

I have already briefly sketched some of the very different interpretations that have been given of *The Castle*. It could be argued that, if one of these is right, either all the rest or some of them must be wrong. And the easy answer to this, that all of them may be right but on different levels, would understandably make many people scream. I would suggest an answer somewhere between these. According to Mr Ronald Gray in his study of *The Castle*, Kafka, unlike the writers of allegory proper, 'studiously avoids equivalents, while at the same time suggesting by an unusual emphasis here or there that more is implied than one is at first aware of '. And Mr Gray goes on: 'To describe one object in terms of another, perhaps the most common device in literature, seems to him like failure. Metaphors, he wrote in his diary, were one of the many things which made him despair about writing.' Yet Mr Gray himself concludes that *The Castle* is 'a description of a metamorphosis of the kind attributed by Christians to the action of grace'. But, whether this interpretation is correct or not, it does surely imply something metaphorical in the book as a whole. Mr Gray suggests that other critics may have gone astray because they treat Kafka as though he were 'a priest or a psychologist who mistook his vocation', whereas Mr Gray —rightly, I think—prefers to treat him 'as a literary artist, not inventing complex equivalents for a system of beliefs already held, but exploring the possibilities of an image which presented itself to his imagination, in this case the image of a castle and of a man trying to reach it'. Now this, as we have seen, seems to have been the procedure—at least at moments—even of a professedly allegorical writer like Spenser. And this is often the procedure when one writes a poem. Which brings me back to the point of 'irreducibility'. Whatever the basic beliefs implicit in *The Castle*, the book cannot be reduced to a mere exposition of such beliefs. If you expound something, that something is not only prior to but more important than the work in which you embody it. Of all the works I have discussed the one that looks nearest to being an exposition, and the one that was most intended to be one, is *Pilgrim's Progress*. But, as I have pointed out more than once, in *Pilgrim's Progress* the story took over: Bunyan was a man of the people, and one occasionally even now finds that when a man of the people is asked for a simple piece of information—such as the way to somewhere or where one can buy a decent rip-saw—he replies by giving you much more than information—sometimes what he gives you is art.

The writer of a mere exposition is not inside what he writes. Bunyan is. So is Kafka. Hence the importance of tone of voice, since tone of voice is individual. And this links up with the more general question of style, which in many of the authors I have discussed—George MacDonald seems to be an exception, not being a good writer *qua* writer —appears to be a constituent of meaning. Kafka said of himself in conversation: 'After all I am a lawyer. So I can never get away from evil.' His whole work can be regarded as the self-examinations of a lawyer haunted by evil, and therefore also haunted by truth. Not only *The Trial*, which from one angle is most obviously a caricature of the Law, but *The Castle* and even a short story like *The Burrow* show an endless and meticulous weighing of pros and cons, the discussion whether one should grant the benefit of the doubt—or its opposite. Thus in both *The Trial* and *The Castle* the people the hero wants to get at—the higher courts, the higher officials—are always at several removes. With this goes the legalistic niggling not only in the dialogue proper—the hero's mistresses also talk like lawyers —but in the hero's self-communings. In the same way in the narrative there is a dry matter-of-factness, a kind of ironic parody of documentary description or ratiocination, that, like Kafka's dialogue, has its parallels in Lewis Carroll and, as in Carroll, serves to underpin the dreamlike mysteries and paradoxes. For an example of this wry dream logic take K. in *The Trial* on his way to his first interrogation. He has been given hardly any directions for finding the interrogation chamber, and discovers that he has to choose between a whole number of staircases: 'his mind played in retrospect with the saying of the warder Willem that an attraction existed between the Law and guilt, from which it should really follow that the interrogation chamber must lie in the particular flight of stairs which K. happened to choose'. This might be called the scholasticism of Angst. It is something we find again in many of Beckett's characters.

To continue the parallel with Carroll (it is mainly, though not entirely, a technical parallel) one can notice in both the same superior attitude on the part of the people encountered and the same indignant reactions on the part of Alice and K. For the setting of a scene I find something Carrollesque in the precise description of the interrogation chamber when K. at last gets into it: 'A crowd of the most variegated people—nobody troubled about the newcomer —filled a medium-sized two-windowed room, which just below the roof was surrounded by a gallery, also quite packed, where the people were able to stand only in a bent posture with their heads and backs knocking against the window.' And for the kind of dialogue where the other party never gets the point, compare the following, also from *The Trial*: '"I see", said K., nodding, "these books are probably law books, and it is an essential part of the justice dispensed here that you should be condemned not only in innocence but in ignorance." "That must be it," said the woman, who had not quite understood him.' To leave Carroll now and make a wider and deeper comparison, half way through *The Trial* there is a scene which recalls the *déjà vu* type of experience so often encountered, not only in dreams, especially perhaps in nightmares, but in traditional fairy stories and in fantasies like those of George Mac-Donald. K. when walking along a corridor in the Bank where he works hears 'convulsive sobs behind a door, which he had always taken to be the door of a lumber-room'. He opens it and sees, among the junk, an unknown man with a rod in his hand, and two others, whom he knows, who are about to be flogged: they explain that it is all K.'s fault. When the flogging and shrieking begin, K. rushes from the room. The next evening 'as he passed the lumber-room again on his way out he could not resist opening the door. And what confronted him . . . bewildered him completely. Everything was still the same, exactly as he had found it on opening the door the previous evening.' So the nightmare comes round again: the Whipper is still there with his two victims and they begin to address him in exactly the same manner.

Mr Goronwy Rees speaks of 'the genuine nobility and grandeur' of Kafka's heroes. This is very unlike Mr Ronald Gray who seems to think that K. in *The Castle* deserves all that comes to him because of something like 'hubris' in his character (I don't think he uses the word but this seems to be what he means). But if K. *has* hubris it is of a very human kind; and this brings me back to the question of 'identification'. It seems to me that in both *The Trial* and *The Castle* the ordinary reader, *qua* Everyman, is bound to identify himself with K. *qua* Everyman, Everyman persecuted or Everyman shut out. Towards the end of *The Trial* there is a parable within a parable and, like the tableaux in the Interpreter's House in *Pilgrim's Progress*, the insert is not only much smaller and more succinct but also, as parable, appears to be more clear-cut. I should underline the word 'appears' since, though K. thinks he understands the fable at once, the priest who relates it to him proceeds, by retailing various conflicting interpretations in vogue among the commentators, to build up a parody of critical exegesis, thereby incidentally anticipating Kafka's own commentators. But here again I side with K. and take the little story as a tragic fable in which the suffering character, like K. himself, has been duped. It is the story of a man from the country who begs for admittance to the 'Law' (the Law here, I suggest, is a wide enough concept to include both Justice and Truth). Before the Law stands a door-keeper on guard. The door-keeper refuses him admission 'at this moment' but gives him a stool and lets him wait. He waits for days and years. Finally his eyes grow dim and he does not know whether the world is really darkening around him or whether his eyes are only deceiving him. But in the darkness he can now perceive a radiance that streams immortally from the door of the Law. Now his life is drawing to a close. So, before it closes, he puts one last question to the door-keeper. 'Everyone', he says, 'strives to attain the Law . . . how does it come about, then, that in all these years no one has come seeking admittance but me?' The door-keeper perceives that the man is at the end of his strength and his hearing is failing, so he bellows in his ear: 'No one but you could gain admittance through this door, since this door was intended only for you. I am now going to shut it.' I have spoken before of 'a spine of allegory' that can lie underneath the softer symbols and the more surface descriptions and decorations. In this magnificent fable I think that spine is showing.

If we can 'identify' with K., we must also identify with the suppliant at the door. But in Kafka's other works I find I can make more improbable identifications. Thus in *Metamorphosis* a young commercial traveller, Gregor Samsa, wakes up one morning to find that he has been turned into a gigantic insect. Some of the more Puritan commentators seem to think that Gregor is being appropriately punished for some failings in himself. I find no internal evidence that Gregor is more deserving of punishment, more insect-like by nature, than any of the characters who retain their human form. The point is surely that Gregor is a misfit and so deserves our sympathy (in his insect form he can understand what his family say but they never suspect this). Herein he is like the misfits in Beckett who do retain human form—but only just. Another short story of Kafka's, *The Burrow*, is told in the first person, like many of Beckett's long soliloquies, and *The Burrow* is also essentially a soliloquy and should hardly be called a story at all. The speaker here is an unspecified small animal, but of a reasoning if selfish kind, which has made itself a most elaborate subterranean labyrinth. This creature is a prey to nagging anxiety. It thinks it is threatened by enemies, 'creatures of the inner earth'; though it has meticulously planned its measures of defence, being both honest and neurotic, it is forced to reflect: 'Here it is of no avail to console yourself with the thought that you are in your own country; for rather are you in theirs.' Can I identify with this selfish anxiety-ridden creature? I think I can. And all this frustration and Angst once more anticipate Beckett.

But there is another thing which Kafka and Beckett have in common. Kafka is reported to have said in conversation: 'What is sin?... We know the word and the practice, but the sense and the knowledge of sin have been lost. Perhaps that is itself damnation, God-forsakenness, meaninglessness.' This obviously anticipates such a novel as *Pincher Martin* by William Golding (which I talk about below). But I think that, though less obviously, it anticipates Beckett too. Beckett's aged and ragged and often crippled soliloquists, senile nostalgia and all, prim obscenity and all, are always trying to be honest with themselves. Which means that they are always looking for themselves and so, *ipso facto*, for that which is not themselves. Their quest is metaphysical. They may not be concerned with God but they are concerned with spiritual meaning, even if all they know about this—or almost all—is its absence. And, though Beckett's characters and probably Beckett himself would not subscribe to Kafka's—or Golding's—concept of sin, their never-ending efforts to answer unanswerable questions seem to imply that they think they have done something wrong, if only through not understanding whatever it is they have done. Perhaps in Beckett the Original Sin is lack of meaning.

I must now confess that I greatly prefer Beckett's plays to his other works: I have by no means read all of the latter, and those that I have read I have not studied very carefully. Some of them, like some of the plays, were written first in French. Esslin explains about the plays that Beckett 'chose to write his masterpieces in French because he needed the discipline that the use of an acquired language would impose on him'. Beckett himself explained that in French it was easier for him to write without style. But style seems to be just the one thing that he does not write without, either in his plays or in his prose works. Beckett's is a beguilingly simple yet subtle style which, as in other cases we have considered where the author was trying to say something peculiar, seems an essential and redeeming part of what he is trying to say. On a first glance at such a prose soliloquy as *Malone Dies* we might be tempted to parody Tennyson and say, 'A dotard crying on the night And with no language but a cry'. After all, Kafka had said that 'for the poet personally his song is only a scream'. Similarly, Mr Laurence Kitchin, when he gave a radio talk on what he called the Compressionist Drama, called it 'The Scream and the Cage', a title drawn from an analogy with the series of paintings of a pope by Francis Bacon. But in all these cases the words 'cry' and 'scream' need qualifying. Beckett's writings may originate in an impulse to cry or scream and in a sense we might say that that is also their total effect. But in a literary work the total effect cannot be summarized in the *terminus ad quem*. One can compare it to an equation: it may end up o = o, but it is all those figures on the way that matter. So a work like *Malone Dies* can no more be reduced to the zero of a mere cry than can Tennyson's *In Memoriam*. It must be admitted that in such prose works Beckett seems often to slip into parody; but then these works, just as much as the plays, are written 'in character': Malone and Molloy and the rest are all character parts. They do not, however, have the rhythm that two or more characters provide, though in *Malone Dies* some differentiation is provided by the stories within the story, the stories which the dying old man tells himself.

A suitable caption for these works of Beckett could be found in an unexpected quarter, in Browning's lines,

> I hardly tried now to rebuke the spring
> My heart made, finding failure in its scope.

Just as the absence of God implies the need of God and therefore the presence of at least something spiritual in man, so to have failed in living implies certain values in living, however much Beckett's characters may curse and blaspheme against it and behave like clowns in a clownish universe. As with any other blasphemy, the other side of the coin is an act of homage. *Malone Dies*, which is acted out, or thought out, or drivelled out on a death-bed, is a good example of all this. It begins: 'I shall soon be quite dead at last in spite of all.' That is, it starts on a note of defiance. And the monstrous old bed-ridden creature goes on: 'I shall be neither hot nor cold any more, I shall be tepid, I shall die tepid, without enthusiasm. . . . I shall not answer any more questions. I shall even try not to ask myself any more.' That is, he continues on a note of reason—at least a kind of reason. And then comes the next sentence: 'While writing, I shall tell myself stories, if I can.' That is, he continues as an artist. And later he adds: 'My desire is henceforward to be clear, without being finical.' Malone is almost 'sans everything', almost a Struldbrug, but, unlike those in Swift, a Struldbrug seen from the inside. And like his creator he is trying to put clearly what is by its nature obscure.

In striking though not complete contrast with my next author, William Golding, Beckett allows almost nothing to happen. Malone is almost as stripped of possessions as Pincher Martin on his rock, and he is equally alone. But

Pincher Martin fights his way to defeat by every kind of delaying action. On what plane he does this is here irrelevant: he is violently hot or violently cold where Malone succeeds in his intention of remaining tepid. Yet they both are as beset by problems as Kafka's creature in *The Burrow*. Malone, however, unlike the other two, treats his with a certain philosophical, almost urbane, and sometimes humorous detachment. Thus when he is entering his last weakness, he comments on it in much the same tone of voice as Alice in Wonderland when faced with her disabilities after drinking from the magic bottle. 'All strains towards the nearest deeps, and notably my feet, which even in the ordinary way are so much further from me than all the rest, from my head I mean, for that is where I am fled, my feet are leagues away.' And then comes the inevitable touch of Irish extravaganza: 'And to call them in, to be cleaned for example, would I think take me over a month, exclusive of the time required to locate them.' Later, when he has lost the hooked stick on which he depends for pushing and pulling things—usually his food and his chamber pot—to and from his bed, he comments on this loss with a series of ironic hyperboles. 'To be buried in lava and not turn a hair, it is then a man shows what stuff he is made of. To know you can do better next time, unrecognizably better, and that there is no next time, and that it is a blessing there is not, there is a thought to be going on with.' The tone is rather like Humpty Dumpty's when he says: 'There's glory for you!' In the next sentence Malone comments drily on his own lost opportunities: 'I thought I was turning my stick to the best possible account, like a monkey scratchings its fleas with the key that opens its cage.' And further down the same page he infers: 'I must have fallen asleep after a brief bout of discouragement, such as I have not experienced for a long time. For why be discouraged, one of the thieves was saved, that is a generous percentage.' The humour here can hardly be called blasphemous, if only because of the implicit compassion—on Beckett's part I mean, not Malone's.

It is a different matter with the love-affair, if so it can be called, of Moll and MacMann: this is one of the last stories that Malone tells himself, and he sets it in some sort of lunatic asylum. MacMann is as monstrously old and decayed as Malone himself while Moll is described as 'a little old woman, immoderately ill-favoured of both face and body. . . . She wore by way of ear-rings two long ivory crucifixes which swayed wildly at the least movement of her head.' To complete the trio of crosses she has within her mouth a single long rotten tooth carved, as Malone says in his typical parody-prose style, 'to represent the celebrated sacrifice'. Neither of these creatures has apparently had a love-affair before, and their attempt to make up for innumerable lost decades is described in deliberately nauseating detail. What is the object of this episode? It is Malone who is telling this story, and Malone's, as I said, is a character part: he has invented 'MacMann', whose name suggests that he too stands for Everyman. And no doubt, in his own impotent and helpless old age, Malone feels entitled to work off on MacMann all the feelings of envy and hatred and disgust that sex may by now be arousing in him (as it aroused them in Swift). But I think there is a further reason, which applies to Beckett as well as to Malone. When Moll first appears Malone comments: 'She seems called on to play a certain part in the remarkable events which, I hope, will enable me to make an end.' This does not only mean an end of the story of MacMann but an end of Malone himself: his stories are a marking time unto death and it looks as if, before he can die, he and Beckett feel that, if only vicariously through his improvised stories, he must go through a purgatory resembling a violent physical purge. Malone's own special catharsis has to be achieved through disgust. But Malone—or Beckett—has the tact not to make this the last episode. 'Moll,' he says (or they say), 'Moll. I'm going to kill her.'

Having got rid of Moll, Malone temporarily drops the story of MacMann and, returning to his own affairs, recounts an unprecedented experience. He has had a visit. His visitor was a mysterious Kafkaesque figure dressed in black with a very tightly rolled umbrella. 'I took him at first for the undertaker's man, annoyed at being called prematurely.' The visitor is never explained and Malone returns to his stories, though admitting that 'all is pretext'. The last story is a light, almost slapstick comedy: a grotesque lady bountiful, called Lady Pedal, insists on taking MacMann and the other loonies out for a picnic in a wagonette. This leads to murder, but by now it is all unreal: MacMann has nearly stopped marking time. This extraordinary piece of prose can as truly be called 'absurd', in Esslin's sense, as any of the plays by Beckett himself or by Genêt or Ionesco. Its apparently inconsequent development and the peculiar convention by which, as it were, a specimen, pickled in a museum in a jar which he cannot see out of, attempts a clinical description not only of himself and the inside of his own jar but also of other specimens all hidden inside their own jars—neither this development or lack of development nor this hardly tenable convention prevents this work being strangely moving. I have spoken often of the 'special worlds' projected by parable writers but, speaking for myself, I do not want any world more special than that—or should I say those?—of *Malone Dies*. For me Beckett's next book, *The Unnamable*, has gone too far. Beckett here seems to have entered the metaphysical territory that we find in the more esoteric Hindu scriptures or in the accounts of the Negative Way given by Christian mystics. A creative writer, I feel, cannot afford to stay long in that territory.

I find it, therefore, a relief to turn to William Golding, where we are back in the world of moralities and story-lines. Golding is far more in the parable tradition than Beckett: it would hardly be a mistake to call him a lineal descendant of Bunyan. Golding's first novel, *The Lord of the Flies*, appeared only in 1954, but already a good deal of criticism has been published about his work, especially, I believe, on the other side of the Atlantic. Most of this I have not read, but I gather that there is more general agreement about the interpretation of his works than there is about Kafka's. I agree on the whole with what Mr John Wain wrote about him in an article entitled 'Lord of the Agonies' in the magazine *Aspect* for April 1963. He described Golding as concerned with the reconciliation of opposites: 'Since he is concerned with extreme situations, this vision of evil is so black that it can only be counterbalanced by a vision of sanctity.' Thus in *Lord of the Flies* the boy Simon is the saint and is, typically, murdered by the other little boys when they lapse into primitive bloodlust. In *The Inheritors* the Neanderthal men are on the whole saintly as compared with the specimens of Homo Sapiens who supersede them. As for *Pincher Martin*, Wain writes that here 'Golding moves on from the Old Testament to the New; from the collective problem of evil in mankind to the drama of the salvation or perdition of an individual soul'. And Golding himself has written of the hero of this great novel: 'Because he was created in the image of God he had a freedom of choice which he used to centre the world on himself. He did not believe in purgatory and therefore when he died it was not presented to him in overtly theological terms. The greed for life which had been the mainspring of his nature forced him to refuse the selfless act of dying. He continued to exist separately in a world composed of his own murderous nature. His drowned body lies rolling in the Atlantic but the ravenous ego invents a rock for him to endure on. It is the memory of an aching tooth.' Wain is correct in describing this and the two earlier novels as 'colossal sculptures in metaphor'—here once again the spine of allegory is no longer latent but patent. I cannot agree with Wain's preference for the fourth and more 'ordinary' novel, *Free Fall*, although, since he says he prefers Shakespeare to Dante, I see his point. Luckily, as we do not have to prefer Shakespeare to the exclusion of Dante or vice versa, so we do not have to exclude one side of Golding if we prefer the other. But it is the Dante side of Golding that is relevant to my present thesis and it is also this side which seems to have made the greater impact.

I will make just a few observations about *Pincher Martin* which may remind the reader of some other parable writers or may illustrate some of my general points about parable writing. To begin with, the title is one of those titles like *The Wild Duck*. In the Navy people called Martin tend to be nicknamed Pincher, just as people called Clark tend to be nicknamed Nobby. But Golding called his hero Martin in order that he should be nicknamed Pincher. As Martin's friend says, he has 'an extraordinary capacity to endure', and as he himself says on the rock, boasting to his unknown adversary: 'I can outwit you. All I have to do is to endure.' And he endures by hanging on, at first with his wits but in the end with his hands alone—alone, that is, except for what is called 'the centre'. The hands are progressively described more and more as if they were lobsters or lobster claws. It is with these claws that he grabs for his own identity. 'I am who I was', he declares, and almost at once we have him sitting, nearly broken, on the edge of a rock trench looking down through what is now called 'the window', and surveying 'all that he could see of himself'. 'There was no body to be seen, only a conjunction of worn materials. He eyed the peculiar shapes that lay across the trousers indifferently for a while, until at last it occurred to him how strange it was that lobsters should sit there. Then he was suddenly seized with a terrible loathing for lobsters and flung them away so that they cracked on the rock. The dull pain of the blow extended him into them again and they became his hands, lying discarded where he had tossed them.' And Golding goes on at once: 'He cleared his throat as if about to speak in public. "How can I have a complete identity without a mirror?"'

A study of the symbolism in *Pincher Martin* would show Golding bringing back his thumping motifs as ruthlessly and tellingly as Beethoven. Apart from the lobster hands there is the rock itself, which is only too much there all through or very, very nearly all through, and every so often there is the tooth image which represents the rock: the rock is as familiar as a remembered missing tooth. Then there is the glass figure floating in the jam-jar and the nightmare image of the cellar, both of these remembered from child-hood: 'and the path from the cellar led to the rock'. And there is the sound of a spade on a tin box, remembered from a drunken friend's ramblings about maggots: 'I am alone on a rock in the middle of a tin box.' Above all there is the image of the 'black lightning', first established in a flashback to Martin's friend lecturing him: 'Take us as we are now and heaven would be sheer negation. Without form and void. You see? A sort of black lightning destroying every-thing that we call life.' In the last apocalyptic scene on the rock it is this very black lightning that destroys first the sea and then all the rock except the part between the claws. But the next moment the rock between the claws is gone too and the claws close upon each other.

All these are obvious symbols and more or less allegorical. But there are a host of other images in this book, all very precise and very physical. We are told in almost unbearable detail how Martin first clambered on to the rock, how he solved the problems of eating and drinking (the sea anemones are described as 'sweets'), how he erected and laid out signals for passing ships and planes, how he finally gave himself a sea-water enema by the ingenious use of his life-belt. Martin, like the heroes of the two earlier novels, exists in a special world which is of necessity a do-it-your-self world. But, as is not the case in the other two novels, the hero here is alone, like Robinson Crusoe or the old man in Hemingway's *The Old Man and the Sea*. Martin is at least as ingenious as those two in solving practical problems and Golding is at least as precise as Hemingway or Defoe in describing how he does this. The important difference is that Martin's practical problems are not, in the literal sense, practical at all, any more than the physical objects, against which he struggles or with which he supports himself, are, in the literal sense, physical at all. For everything that happens on the rock is a symbol just like the rock itself. There have been readers whom the wealth of physical detail and the very vivid account of Martin's struggle for survival have tricked into taking this struggle literally and who have accordingly been disappointed by the last chapter which makes it clear, though it should have been clear before, that such a struggle never took place. But this epilogue, though perhaps unnecessary, in no way invalidates what has gone before. What Golding is recounting is a story like *Pilgrim's Progress*. And, whatever the views of either Golding or the reader about either God or personal immortality, morally and metaphysically the story is valid and the question, for example, of duration is irrelevant. The story is so long and so detailed—in the world of symbol Martin spends days and nights on the rock—that it is a natural reaction for a reader brought up on realism to complain that this is an unconvincing way of representing an almost sudden death. A natural reaction but irrelevant. Even if one believes that death is the absolute end, one must recognize that the issues involved in death, which retrospectively cover a man's life, can be spread by the parable writer on any size of canvas he chooses. If one were a medieval scholastic one might now ask: 'How many devils can dance on the point of a pin?' William Golding—and I mean something more than a pun here—has certainly pinpointed the issues on his Rock.

Golding seems a good writer with whom to end this survey. He is more in the tradition than Beckett; he is also the kind of writer that we probably need more. *Pincher Martin* is the twentieth-century *Peer Gynt*. 'When am I going to get to the heart?' said Peer as he peeled the onion. Pincher Martin, like many of the heroes in modern parable writing, is much concerned with his own identity. Golding, as ruthlessly as most of the other authors, strips this away from him. But even Beckett, as I suggested just now, leaves to his characters, if only by paradox, not an escape perhaps but a kind of indication. If you strip the onion to pieces you will probably not find a heart. But, if you know all those layers upon layers, you may with luck put the onion together again; this is not possible in horticulture but it is, I suggest, both in art and in human life. All good parable writers are concerned with truth, and it often is the kind of truth that cannot be, or can hardly be, expressed in other ways.

BIBLIOGRAPHY

This bibliography includes some of the works of criticism referred to by Mr MacNeice in his lectures.

Auden, W. H. *The Enchafèd Flood*. London, 1951.

Damon, S. F., Raine, K., *et al. The Divine Vision: Studies in the Poetry and Art of William Blake*. London, 1957.

Esslin, M. *The Theatre of the Absurd*. London, 1962.

Frye, N. *The Anatomy of Criticism*. Princeton, 1957.

Gray, R. *Kafka's Castle*. Cambridge, 1956.

Honig, E. *The Dark Conceit*. London, 1960.

Hough, G. G. *A Preface to the Faerie Queene*. London, 1962.

House, H. *Coleridge* (Clark Lectures 1951–2). London, 1953.

Lewis, C. S. *The Allegory of Love*. Oxford, 1936.

Northam, J. R. *Ibsen's Dramatic Method*. London, 1953.

Spens, J. *Spenser's Faerie Queene: An Interpretation*. London, 1934.

Tuve, R. *A Reading of George Herbert*. London, 1952.

Weston, J. L. *From Ritual to Romance*. Cambridge, 1920.

INDEX

'Absurd', theatre and playwrights of, *see* Esslin, Martin, *also* Beckett, Ionesco, Pinter

Aesop, fables of, 1

allegory: discarded as a title-word, 1, 2; definitions of, 3–5, 16–17; and symbolism, 4–5, 16–17, 52–4, 59, 64, 66–7, 75, 94; supplies subjective element in literature, 5, 52; 'naïve', 17, 76, 129; 'proper', 18; free-style, 18; modern critical interest in, 26–7; ambiguity in modern, 28; variety in Spenser's, 33–41; Herbert's, 50; in folk ballads, 65–6; in Andersen, 74–5; in Carroll, 90–4; author's experience of writing, 111–12; *see also* parable

Amis, Kingsley, 1–2

Andersen, Hans, 7; as allegorist, 74–5; similarities with Arnold, 80, with Kingsley, 87; pioneer of writing for children, 82

Arnold, Matthew, *Forsaken Merman*, 79–80

attitude, a formalizing element in creative literature, 20–2

Auden, W. H., on allegory and symbolism, 53, 75; on Romantic attitude to sea, 84; verges on parable in *The Age of Anxiety*, 106–7

Austen, Jane, 12

Barrie, J. M., in *Peter Pan*, 85, 101, 102

Beckett, Samuel, 4, 5, 13, 24, 26, 28; preoccupied with 'nothingness', 14, 60; his style, 16, 140–2; marks *ne plus ultra* in parable, 25; comparable with Blake, 60, with Carroll, 120–1,

143, with Simpson, 121; and absence of character and plot, 119–20; and search for truth or identity, 123–4, 140; his use of silence, 128–9

Endgame, 15, 51, 60, 128; 'quest' theme in, 119; compared with *Alice* books, 120–1

Krapp's Last Tape, 23

Malone Dies, 16, 77, 141–6

The Unnamable, 128, 146

Waiting for Godot, 2; similar to folk tale, 12; 'identification' with characters of, 22–3; multiple correspondences in, 54, 113; Esslin on, 117; 'quest' theme in, 119–20

belief; a formalizing element in creative writing, 19–22; and unbelief, 118

Bergman, Ingmar, 9–10

Blake, William, 13, 16, 18; on *Pilgrim's Progress*, 53–4; Kathleen Raine on 'archetypes' in, 55, 56, 95; an unconscious neo-Platonist, 59–60; a natural visionary, 65

Book of Thel, The: author's appreciation of, 54–5, 57–9; Kathleen Raine on, 56; Damon on, 56–7, 58–9

Brecht, Bertolt, his 'alienation' principle, 22, 29, 119

Brod, Max, 122

Browne, Sir Thomas, 47

Browning, Robert, 3; *Childe Roland* his one parable, 71–2, 79, 80–2

Bunyan, John, 5, 6, 12; essentially evangelical, 20, 43; naturalistic dialogue in, 23, 41–2; medieval elements in, 43; his sleight-of-hand writing, 45; his prose style, 47–8, 49